מעובדה

ArtScroll Mesorah Series®

Expositions on Jewish liturgy and thought

Rabbis Nosson Scherman / Meir Zlotowitz
General Editors

*A Haggadah with extensive commentary
and an introductory essay is available as part
of the* ARTSCROLL SERIES.
*The Series includes original translations
and commentaries on books of the
Bible, Mishnah, Jewish liturgy and thought.
The ArtScroll Series is available
at Judaica booksellers or directly from
the publisher.*

The Family
Haggadah

הגדה של פסח

Haggadah

Published by

Mesorah Publications, ltd

The Family

Translation and Introduction by
Rabbi Nosson Scherman

Marginal notes by
Rabbi Avie Gold

Designed and Produced by
Sheah Brander

FIRST EDITION

Seventeen Impressions . . . January 1981-December 1997
Eighteenth Impression . . . February 1999
Nineteenth Impression . . . January 2001

Published and Distributed by
MESORAH PUBLICATIONS, Ltd.
4401 Second Avenue
Brooklyn, New York 11232

Distributed in Europe by
LEHMANNS
Unit E, Viking Industrial Park
Rolling Mill Road
Jarrow, Tyne & Wear NE32 3DP
England

Distributed in Australia & Zew Zealand by
GOLDS WORLD OF JUDAICA
3-13 William Street
Balaclava, Melbourne 3183
Victoria Australia

Distributed in Israel by
SIFRIATI / A. GITLER — BOOKS
6 Hayarkon Street
Bnei Brak 51127

Distributed in South Africa by
KOLLEL BOOKSHOP
Shop 8A Norwood Hypermarket
Norwood 2196, Johannesburg, South Africa

THE FAMILY HAGGADAH ®
© Copyright 1981, 1994 by MESORAH PUBLICATIONS, Ltd.
4401 Second Avenue / Brooklyn, N.Y. 11232 / (718) 921-9000 / www.artscroll.com

All rights reserved. This text, the new translation, commentary, and prefatory comments
— including the typographic layout, illustrations, charts, appendices, and cover design —
have been edited and revised as to content, form and style
and are fully protected against copyright infringement.

No part of this book may be reproduced
in any form — including photocopying and retrieval systems —
without **written** permission from the copyright holder,
except by a reviewer who wishes to quote brief passages in connection with a review
written for inclusion in magazines or newspapers.

THE RIGHTS OF THE COPYRIGHT HOLDER WILL BE STRICTLY ENFORCED.

ISBN: 0-89906-178-8 (paperback only)

Typography by CompuScribe at ArtScroll Studios, Ltd.
4401 Second Avenue / Brooklyn, N.Y. 11232 / (718) 921-9000
Printed in the United States of America by Noble Book Press

Table of Contents

◄§ Introduction

The Seder/A Celebration of Freedom and Family   9

◄§ Preparing for Passover

The Search for Chametz   13

Burning the Chametz   14

Eruv Tavshilin   15

Lighting the Candles   16

◄§ The Seder

The Seder Plate   18

The Order of the Seder   19

The Haggadah   20

Shir HaShirim / Song of Songs   93

❧ The Seder /
A Celebration of Freedom and Family

Hardly a ceremony in Jewish life is more familiar and more widely observed than the Passover Seder. For countless grandparents and parents, it represents an "ingathering of exiles" of sorts, as children converge from far and wide to celebrate the Seder together. Indeed, the family aspect of the Seder is an integral part of the observance, for the Torah speaks frequently of the responsibility of parents to teach their children about the Exodus.

The family aspect of the Seder is an integral part of the observance, for the Torah speaks frequently of the responsibility of parents to teach their children about the Exodus.

Of no other commandment does the Torah speak about children's questions and parents' answers. So when the littlest member of the household is coaxed, bribed, and encouraged to stand before Zaidy or Daddy and say the *Mah Nishtanah,* the heartwarming ritual is truly an essential part of the Seder — for this is a night when bonds are forged between parent and child, when the chain of generations is strengthened and new links are added. It is a night when, as we say in the Haggadah, every Jew should regard himself as though *he* were freed from Egyptian slavery, and began the march from the land of his bondage toward Sinai, where Israel would receive the gift of the Ten Commandments.

This is a night when bonds are forged between parent and child, when the chain of generations is strengthened and new links are added.

So important is that aspect of the interraction between parent and child that the Sages instituted

9 □ THE FAMILY HAGGADAH

some Seder customs primarily to stimulate the curiosity of youngsters. Let them ask. Let their parents answer. Let everyone inquire, think, delve, innovate, find ways to relate the adventure of old to the challenges of today. For the Seder and its narrative speak to every generation. Every era has its Egypt, its own brand of slavery and temptation that inhibits the development of Israel. And to every generation, the Seder says that this night *is* different, because it brings home lessons that can easily be drowned in the constant activity of daily life.

Every era has its Egypt, its own brand of slavery and temptation that inhibits the development of Israel. And to every generation, the Seder says that this night is different

The Talmud lays down the dictum that our narrative of freedom must begin with the tale of our degradation, for it is only when someone recalls how bad things *were* that he can realize how good things *are*. The Haggadah's narrative of the torturous slavery of Egypt is understandable — that was bondage in its most literal sense. Surely freedom must have been sweet to the Jew whose back still smarted from the scars of a taskmaster's whip, to the mother whose child had been bricked into a pyramid or drowned in the Nile.

Surely freedom must have been sweet to the Jew whose back still smarted from the scars of the taskmaster's whip

But the Haggadah contains a second narrative of degradation and our escape from it: *Originally our ancestors were idol worshipers, but now the Omnipresent has brought us near to His service.* There is another slavery, another degradation, one that is *not* to masters holding whips, enforcing production quotas, murdering children, separating families. Idolatry, too, is a form of enslavement, for when people choose idols that suit their own desires and concerns, they are truly slaves — to their own passions. Our ancestors were pagans. As pagans they were spiritually flawed and they would have passed on their spiritual blemish to their posterity, had not Israel been liberated from this slavery to codes of man's own creation.

Idolatry, too, is a form of enslavement, for when people choose idols that suit their own desires and concerns, they are truly slaves — to their own passions.

So the Exodus represented a two-fold liberation: from physical enslavement and from spiritual degradation. The nation as a whole was cleansed of both blemishes. On the night of Passover it came to acknowledge no master but God and it began the trek to the Wilderness where it would stand at Sinai

הגדה של פסח □ 10

Are the enslavement of Pharaoh and the idolatry of Terach behind us? The Seder is not only a celebration of past liberation but also a challenge to retain it.

and declare its willingness to accept the privilege of bearing God's message of truth and morality.

Are the enslavement of Pharaoh and the idolatry of Terach behind us? Hardly. History books and newspapers alike illustrate all too vividly that physical independence is easily lost and moral freedom easily subverted. The Seder is not only a celebration of past liberation but also a challenge to retain it. That is why we declare the responsibility of every Jewish man, woman, and child to regard himself or herself as one of those hundreds of thousands who departed Egypt for a better life and a greater responsibility. Only by understanding the past and identifying with it can we deal intelligently with the future. Terach tried to impose idolatry on his children — so he was our enemy. Laban tried to wean his grandchildren, the first totally Jewish family, away from the faith of Abraham, Isaac, and Jacob — so he was our enemy. Pharaoh tried to destroy Jewish nationhood and try to assimilate it into the Egyptian people — so he was our enemy. These were different kinds of challenges and one or the other is a mirror of virtually every danger — bitter or sweet — that has ever confronted Israel.

Therefore we gather our generations around the Seder table and transmit the message of Jewish history to our children. According to the Halachah, the Seder narrative must be understood; indeed, the great scholars of Jewish history made it a point to translate and simplify the Haggadah so that everyone at their tables could understand. As the Haggadah tells us, the greatest sages of their time gathered in Bnei Brak to discuss the redemption and its implications for them. And as the Haggadah tells us, the Seder night is the time to relate to our children — from the wisest to the simplest — encouraging them to ask, inquire, challenge, learn; for only by doing so can they become part of Jewish history and make it part of their own personal experience and perspective of the world.

According to Halachah, the Seder night is the time to relate to our children, encouraging them to ask, inquire, challenge, learn.

The Seder is a celebration of history — the past *and* the future. Though we Jews always learn from our past, we simultaneously look ahead to a future of spiritual perfection. This is symbolized by the Hallel prayer of the Seder. The first two chapters of Hallel refer to the miracles of the Exodus; they are recited just before the Seder feast. Following the festive meal with its many *mitzvos*, we continue with the rest of Hallel, the ecstatic songs of hope and prayer that allude to the prophetic visions of plowshares taking the place of swords and of Jerusalem displacing the martial capitals of the world.

Let us hear its message of the past and let it teach us how to order our present that we may build a better future.

Let us gather up our children and ourselves, to begin the Seder. Let us hear its message of the past and let it teach us how to order our present that we may build a better future.

הגדה של פסח ☐ 12

✍ Preparing for Passover

בדיקת
חמץ

The
Search
for
Chametz

Aside from the commandment to eat matzah all of Passover and the special observances of the Seder nights, the best-known feature of the festival is the requirement not to eat, or even to own, chametz all during the festival. For many Jews, one of the most vivid memories of their childhood is the seemingly endless cleaning and scrubbing of their homes during the weeks and days before Passover.

Although no household can be thoroughly cleaned in only a short while, the Talmudic Sages ordained that a search for chametz be made in every home and business on one night of the year.

The search begins upon nightfall of the fourteenth day of Nissan, the evening before Passover. The purpose of the commandment is the removal of all chametz, and it requires a formal inspection of all areas where chametz may have been brought during the course of the year — despite the fact that a thorough cleaning was made before Passover. The search should be made by candlelight, and one may not speak until it is completed — except to give instructions or make inquiries directly relating to the search.

In years when Passover begins on Saturday night, the inspection is not conducted on the evening before Passover, for this would result in a desecration of the Sabbath. Instead, it is made on Thursday night and the chametz is burned Friday morning.

A widespread custom calls for the distribution of ten pieces of chametz through the house before the search (by someone other than the person conducting the search). Of course, care should be taken that the pieces do not leave crumbs, thereby defeating the purpose of the search.

Any chametz intended for that evening's supper or the next morning's breakfast must be set aside carefully. After eating, leftover chametz should be placed with whatever chametz may have been found in the evening. They will be burned the morning before Passover (except when Passover begins on Saturday night, in which case the chametz is burned Friday morning).

13 ☐ THE FAMILY HAGGADAH

The chametz search is initiated with the recitation of the following blessing:

בָּרוּךְ אַתָּה יהוה אֱלֹהֵינוּ מֶלֶךְ הָעוֹלָם אֲשֶׁר קִדְּשָׁנוּ בְּמִצְוֹתָיו וְצִוָּנוּ עַל בִּעוּר חָמֵץ:

Blessed are You, HASHEM, our God, King of the universe, Who has sanctified us by His commandments, and commanded us concerning the removal of Chametz.

Upon completion of the chametz search, the chametz is wrapped well and set aside to be burned the next morning and the following declaration is made. The declaration must be understood in order to take effect; one who does not understand the Aramaic text may recite it in English, Yiddish or any other language. Any chametz that will be used for that evening's supper or the next day's breakfast or for any other purpose prior to the final removal of chametz the next morning is not included in this declaration.

כָּל חֲמִירָא וַחֲמִיעָא דְּאִכָּא בִרְשׁוּתִי דְּלָא חֲמִתֵּהּ וּדְלָא בִעַרְתֵּהּ וּדְלָא יָדַעְנָא לֵיהּ לִבְטֵל וְלֶהֱוֵי הֶפְקֵר כְּעַפְרָא דְּאַרְעָא:

Any Chametz which is in my possession which I did not see, and remove, nor know about, shall be nullified and become ownerless, like the dust of the earth.

The following declaration, which includes all chametz without exception, is to be made after the burning of leftover chametz. It should be recited in a language which one understands. When Passover begins on Saturday night, this declaration is made on Saturday morning. Any chametz remaining from the Saturday morning meal, is flushed down the drain before the declaration is made.

כָּל חֲמִירָא וַחֲמִיעָא דְּאִכָּא בִרְשׁוּתִי דַּחֲזִתֵּהּ וּדְלָא חֲזִתֵּהּ דַּחֲמִתֵּהּ וּדְלָא חֲמִתֵּהּ דְּבִעַרְתֵּהּ וּדְלָא בִעַרְתֵּהּ לִבְטֵל וְלֶהֱוֵי הֶפְקֵר כְּעַפְרָא דְּאַרְעָא:

ביעור חמץ

Burning the Chametz

הגדה של פסח □ 14

Any Chametz which is in my possession which I did or did not see, which I did or did not remove, shall be nullified and become ownerless, like the dust of the earth.

עירוב תבשילין

Eruv Tavshilin

It is forbidden to prepare on Yom Tov for the next day even if that day is the Sabbath. If, however, Sabbath preparations were started before Yom Tov began, they may be continued on Yom Tov. Eruv Tavshilin constitutes this preparation. A matzah and any cooked food (such as fish, meat, or an egg) are set aside on the day before Yom Tov to be used on the Sabbath and the blessing is recited followed by the declaration [made in a language understood by the one making the Eruv].

If the first days of Passover fall on Thursday and Friday, an Eruv Tavshilin must be made on Wednesday.

In Eretz Yisrael, where only one day Yom Tov is in effect, the Eruv is omitted.

בָּרוּךְ אַתָּה יהוה אֱלֹהֵינוּ מֶלֶךְ הָעוֹלָם אֲשֶׁר קִדְּשָׁנוּ בְּמִצְוֹתָיו וְצִוָּנוּ עַל־ מִצְוַת עֵרוּב:

Blessed are You, HASHEM, our God, King of the universe, Who sanctified us by His commandments and commanded us concerning the commandment of Eruv.

בְּהָדֵין עֵרוּבָא יְהֵא שָׁרֵא לָנָא לַאֲפוּיֵי וּלְבַשׁוּלֵי וּלְאַצְלוּיֵי וּלְאַטְמוּנֵי וּלְאַדְלוּקֵי שְׁרָגָא וּלְתַקָּנָא וּלְמֶעְבַּד כָּל צָרְכָנָא מִיּוֹמָא טָבָא לְשַׁבַּתָּא לָנוּ וּלְכָל יִשְׂרָאֵל הַדָּרִים בָּעִיר הַזֹּאת:

Through this Eruv may we be permitted to bake, cook, fry, insulate, kindle flame, prepare for, and do anything necessary on the festival for the sake of the Sabbath — for ourselves and for all Jews who live in this city.

הדלקת הנרות
Lighting the Candles

The candles are lit and the following blessings are recited. When Yom Tov falls on the Sabbath, the words in parentheses are added.

בָּרוּךְ אַתָּה יהוה אֱלֹהֵינוּ מֶלֶךְ הָעוֹלָם אֲשֶׁר קִדְּשָׁנוּ בְּמִצְוֹתָיו וְצִוָּנוּ לְהַדְלִיק נֵר שֶׁל (שַׁבָּת וְשֶׁל) יוֹם טוֹב:

Blessed are You, HASHEM, our God, King of the universe, Who has sanctified us through His commandments, and commanded us to kindle the flame of the (Sabbath and the) festival.

בָּרוּךְ אַתָּה יהוה אֱלֹהֵינוּ מֶלֶךְ הָעוֹלָם שֶׁהֶחֱיָנוּ וְקִיְּמָנוּ וְהִגִּיעָנוּ לַזְּמַן הַזֶּה:

Blessed are You, HASHEM, our God, King of the universe, Who has kept us alive, sustained us, and brought us to this season.

הגדה של פסח □ 16

8 The Seder

❧ The Seder Plate

The Seder preparations should be made in time for the Seder to begin as soon as the synagogue services are finished. It should not begin before nightfall, however. Matzah, bitter herbs and several other items of symbolic significance are placed on the Seder plate in the arrangement shown below.

ג' מצות
3 MATZOS

Matzah — Three whole matzos are placed one atop the other, separated by a cloth or napkin. Matzah must be eaten three times during the Seder, by itself, with maror, and as the afikoman. Each time, the minimum portion of matzah for each person should have a volume equivalent to half an egg. Where many people are present, enough matzos should be available to enable each participant to receive a proper portion.

Maror and **Chazeres** — Bitter herbs are eaten twice during the Seder, once by themselves and a second time with matzah. Each time a minimum portion, equal to the volume of half an egg should be eaten. The Talmud lists several vegetables that qualify as Maror, two of which are put on the Seder plate in the places marked Chazeres and Maror. Most people use romaine lettuce (whole leaves or stalks) for Chazeres, and horseradish (whole or grated) for Maror, although either may be used for the mitzvah of eating Maror later in the Seder.

Charoses — The bitter herbs are dipped into charoses (a mixture of grated apples, nuts, other fruit, cinnamon and other spices, mixed with red wine). The charoses has the appearance of mortar to symbolize the lot of the Hebrew slaves, whose lives were embittered by hard labor with brick and mortar.

Z'roa [Roasted bone] and **Beitzah** [Roasted Egg] — On the eve of Passover in the Holy Temple in Jerusalem, two sacrifices were offered and their meat roasted and eaten at the Seder feast. To commemorate these two sacrifices we place a roasted bone (with some meat on it) and a roasted hard-boiled egg on the Seder plate.

The egg, a symbol of mourning, is used in place of a second piece of meat as a reminder of our mourning at the destruction of the Temple — may it be rebuilt speedily in our day.

Karpas — A vegetable (celery, parsley, boiled potato) other than bitter herbs completes the Seder plate. It will be dipped in salt water and eaten. (The salt water is not put on the Seder plate, but it, too, should be prepared beforehand, and placed near the Seder plate).

❧ The Order of the Seder

*The Seder ritual contains fifteen observances, which have been summarized in the familiar rhyme **Kaddesh, Urechatz, Karpas, Yachatz,** and so on. Aside from its convenience as a memory device, the brief formula has been given various deeper interpretations over the years. Accordingly, many people recite the appropriate word from the rhyme before performing the mitzvah to which it applies — קַדֵּשׁ, Kaddesh, before Kiddush, וּרְחַץ, Urechatz, before washing the hands, and so on.*

KADDESH	**Sanctify** the day with the recitation of Kiddush.	קדש
URECHATZ	**Wash** the hands before eating Karpas.	ורחץ
KARPAS	Eat a **vegetable** dipped in salt water.	כרפס
YACHATZ	**Break** the middle matzah. Put away larger half for Afikoman	יחץ
MAGGID	**Narrate** the story of the Exodus from Egypt.	מגיד
RACHTZAH	**Wash** the hands prior to the meal.	רחצה
MOTZI	Recite the blessing, **Who brings forth**, over matzah as a food.	מוציא
MATZAH	Recite the blessing over **Matzah**.	מצה
MAROR	Recite the blessing for the eating of the **bitter herbs.**	מרור
KORECH	Eat the **sandwich** of matzah and bitter herbs.	כורך
SHULCHAN ORECH	The **table prepared** with the festive meal.	שלחן עורך
TZAFUN	Eat the afikoman which had been **hidden** all during the Seder.	צפון
BARECH	Recite Bircas Hamazon, the **blessings** after the meal.	ברך
HALLEL	Recite the **Hallel** Psalms of praise	הלל
NIRTZAH	Pray that God **accept** our observance and speedily send the Messiah.	נרצה

קַדֵּשׁ

Kiddush should be recited and the Seder begun as soon after synagogue services as possible—however, not before nightfall. Each participant's cup should be poured by someone else to symbolize the majesty of the evening, as though each participant had a servant.

On Friday night begin here:

וַיְהִי עֶרֶב וַיְהִי בֹקֶר

יוֹם הַשִּׁשִּׁי: וַיְכֻלּוּ הַשָּׁמַיִם וְהָאָרֶץ וְכָל צְבָאָם: וַיְכַל אֱלֹהִים בַּיּוֹם הַשְּׁבִיעִי מְלַאכְתּוֹ אֲשֶׁר עָשָׂה וַיִּשְׁבֹּת בַּיּוֹם הַשְּׁבִיעִי מִכָּל מְלַאכְתּוֹ אֲשֶׁר עָשָׂה: וַיְבָרֶךְ אֱלֹהִים אֶת יוֹם הַשְּׁבִיעִי וַיְקַדֵּשׁ אֹתוֹ כִּי בוֹ שָׁבַת מִכָּל מְלַאכְתּוֹ אֲשֶׁר בָּרָא אֱלֹהִים לַעֲשׂוֹת:

On all nights other than Friday, begin here;
on Friday night include all passages in parentheses.

סַבְרִי מָרָנָן וְרַבָּנָן וְרַבּוֹתַי:

בָּרוּךְ אַתָּה יהוה אֱלֹהֵינוּ מֶלֶךְ הָעוֹלָם בּוֹרֵא פְּרִי הַגָּפֶן:

בָּרוּךְ אַתָּה יהוה אֱלֹהֵינוּ מֶלֶךְ הָעוֹלָם אֲשֶׁר בָּחַר בָּנוּ מִכָּל עָם וְרוֹמְמָנוּ מִכָּל לָשׁוֹן וְקִדְּשָׁנוּ בְּמִצְוֹתָיו. וַתִּתֶּן לָנוּ יהוה אֱלֹהֵינוּ בְּאַהֲבָה (שַׁבָּתוֹת לִמְנוּחָה וּ)מוֹעֲדִים לְשִׂמְחָה חַגִּים וּזְמַנִּים לְשָׂשׂוֹן אֶת יוֹם (הַשַּׁבָּת הַזֶּה וְאֶת יוֹם) חַג הַמַּצּוֹת הַזֶּה זְמַן חֵרוּתֵנוּ (בְּאַהֲבָה) מִקְרָא קֹדֶשׁ זֵכֶר לִיצִיאַת מִצְרָיִם. כִּי בָנוּ בָחַרְתָּ וְאוֹתָנוּ קִדַּשְׁתָּ מִכָּל הָעַמִּים (וְשַׁבָּת)

הגדה של פסח □ 20

KADDESH

The holiness of the day is proclaimed by the recitation of Kiddush.

Kiddush should be recited and the Seder begun as soon after synagogue services as possible—however, not before nightfall. Each participant's cup should be poured by someone else to symbolize the majesty of the evening, as though each participant had a servant.

On Friday night begin here:

(And there was evening and there was morning)

[Although the night's proceedings focus on the Exodus, the Sabbath Kiddush takes precedence for it is the more common occurrence, and it commemorates an earlier event, the Creation.]

The sixth day. Thus the heaven and the earth were finished, and all their array. On the seventh day God completed His work which He had done, and He abstained on the seventh day from all His work which He had done. God blessed the seventh day and hallowed it, because on it He abstained from all His work which God created to make (Genesis 1:31-2:3).

On all nights other than Friday, begin here;
on Friday night include all passages in parentheses.

By your leave, my masters and teachers:

Blessed are You, HASHEM, our God, King of the universe, Who creates the fruit of the vine.

Blessed are You, HASHEM, our God, King of the universe, Who has chosen us from all nations, exalted us above all tongues, and sanctified us with His commandments. And You, HASHEM, our God, have lovingly given us (Sabbaths for rest), appointed times for gladness, feasts and seasons for joy, (this Sabbath and) this Feast of Matzos, the season of our freedom (in love,) a holy convocation in memoriam of the Exodus from Egypt. For You have chosen and sanctified us above all peoples, (and the Sabbath) and Your holy festivals (in

God has sanctified us with His commandments, and we, in turn, sanctify Time by our fulfillment of His will.

21 □ THE FAMILY HAGGADAH

וּמוֹעֲדֵי קָדְשֶׁךָ (בְּאַהֲבָה וּבְרָצוֹן) בְּשִׂמְחָה וּבְשָׂשׂוֹן הִנְחַלְתָּנוּ. בָּרוּךְ אַתָּה יהוה מְקַדֵּשׁ (הַשַּׁבָּת וְ) יִשְׂרָאֵל וְהַזְּמַנִּים:

On Saturday night, add the following two paragraphs:

בָּרוּךְ אַתָּה יהוה אֱלֹהֵינוּ מֶלֶךְ הָעוֹלָם בּוֹרֵא מְאוֹרֵי הָאֵשׁ:

בָּרוּךְ אַתָּה יהוה אֱלֹהֵינוּ מֶלֶךְ הָעוֹלָם הַמַּבְדִּיל בֵּין קֹדֶשׁ לְחוֹל בֵּין אוֹר לְחֹשֶׁךְ בֵּין יִשְׂרָאֵל לָעַמִּים בֵּין יוֹם הַשְּׁבִיעִי לְשֵׁשֶׁת יְמֵי הַמַּעֲשֶׂה. בֵּין קְדֻשַּׁת שַׁבָּת לִקְדֻשַּׁת יוֹם טוֹב הִבְדַּלְתָּ וְאֶת יוֹם הַשְּׁבִיעִי מִשֵּׁשֶׁת יְמֵי הַמַּעֲשֶׂה קִדַּשְׁתָּ. הִבְדַּלְתָּ וְקִדַּשְׁתָּ אֶת עַמְּךָ יִשְׂרָאֵל בִּקְדֻשָּׁתֶךָ. בָּרוּךְ אַתָּה יהוה הַמַּבְדִּיל בֵּין קֹדֶשׁ לְקֹדֶשׁ:

On all nights conclude here:

בָּרוּךְ אַתָּה יהוה אֱלֹהֵינוּ מֶלֶךְ הָעוֹלָם שֶׁהֶחֱיָנוּ וְקִיְּמָנוּ וְהִגִּיעָנוּ לַזְּמַן הַזֶּה:

The wine should be drunk without delay while reclining on the left side. It is preferable to drink the entire cup, but at the very least, most of the cup should be drained.

The head of the household — according to many opinions, all participants in the Seder — washes his hands as if to eat bread, [pouring water from a cup, twice on the right hand and twice on the left] but without reciting a blessing.

כרפס

All participants take a vegetable other than maror and dip it into salt-water. A piece smaller in volume than half an egg should be used. The following blessing is recited [with the intention that it also applies to the marror which will be eaten during the meal] before the vegetable is eaten.

בָּרוּךְ אַתָּה יהוה אֱלֹהֵינוּ מֶלֶךְ הָעוֹלָם בּוֹרֵא פְּרִי הָאֲדָמָה:

הגדה של פסח ☐ 22

love and favor), in gladness and joy have You granted us as a heritage. Blessed are You, HASHEM, Who sanctifies (the Sabbath,) Israel, and the festive seasons.

On Saturday night, add the following two paragraphs:

Blessed are You, HASHEM, our God, King of the universe, Who creates the illumination of the fire.

Blessed are You, HASHEM, our God, King of the universe, Who distinguishes between sacred and secular, between light and darkness, between Israel and the nations, between the seventh day and the six days of activity. You have distinguished between the holiness of the Sabbath and the holiness of a Festival, and have sanctified the seventh day above the six days of activity. You distinguished and sanctified Your nation, Israel, with Your holiness. Blessed are You, HASHEM, Who distinguishes between holiness and holiness.

On all nights conclude here:

Blessed are You, HASHEM, our God, King of the universe, Who has kept us alive, sustained us, and brought us to this season.

The wine should be drunk without delay while reclining on the left side. It is preferable to drink the entire cup, but at the very least, most of the cup should be drained.

URECHATZ

The head of the household — according to many opinions, all participants in the Seder — washes his hands as if to eat bread, [pouring water from a cup, twice on the right hand and twice on the left] but without reciting a blessing.

KARPAS

All participants take a vegetable other than maror and dip it into salt-water. A piece smaller in volume than half an egg should be used. The following blessing is recited [with the intention that it also applies to the marror which will be eaten during the meal] before the vegetable is eaten.

The vegetable used for Karpas is of lowly origin, from beneath the earth. Yet, it develops into an integral part of a sacred feast. So the lowly slave-nation grew to become the Chosen People. And so must each Jew, regardless of background, strive for ever greater spiritual heights.

Blessed are You, HASHEM, our God, King of the universe, Who creates the fruit of the earth.

23 □ THE FAMILY HAGGADAH

The head of the household breaks the middle matzah in two. He puts the smaller part back between the two whole matzos, and wraps up the larger part for later use as the Afikoman. Some briefly place the Afikoman portion on their shoulders, in accordance with the Biblical verse recounting that Israel left Egypt carrying their matzos on their shoulders, and say בְּבֶהָלוּ יָצָאנוּ מִמִּצְרַיִם, 'In haste we went out of Egypt.'

The broken matzah is lifted for all to see as the head of the household begins with the following brief explanation of the proceedings.

הָא לַחְמָא עַנְיָא דִי אֲכָלוּ אַבְהָתָנָא בְּאַרְעָא דְמִצְרָיִם. כָּל דִּכְפִין יֵיתֵי וְיֵכוֹל כָּל דִּצְרִיךְ יֵיתֵי וְיִפְסַח. הָשַׁתָּא הָכָא לְשָׁנָה הַבָּאָה בְּאַרְעָא דְיִשְׂרָאֵל. הָשַׁתָּא עַבְדֵי לְשָׁנָה הַבָּאָה בְּנֵי חוֹרִין:

The Seder plate is removed and the second of the four cups of wine is poured. The youngest present asks the reasons for the unusual proceedings of the evening.

מַה נִּשְׁתַּנָּה הַלַּיְלָה הַזֶּה מִכָּל הַלֵּילוֹת?

שֶׁבְּכָל הַלֵּילוֹת אָנוּ אוֹכְלִין חָמֵץ וּמַצָּה הַלַּיְלָה הַזֶּה כֻּלּוֹ מַצָּה.

שֶׁבְּכָל הַלֵּילוֹת אָנוּ אוֹכְלִין שְׁאָר יְרָקוֹת הַלַּיְלָה הַזֶּה מָרוֹר.

YACHATZ

A matzah is broken and set aside for later use. The redemption is at this moment incomplete, we are free from Egypt, but ...

The head of the household breaks the middle matzah in two. He puts the smaller part back between the two whole matzos, and wraps up the larger part for later use as the Afikoman. Some briefly place the Afikoman portion on their shoulders, in accordance with the Biblical verse recounting that Israel left Egypt carrying their matzos on their shoulders, and say בְּבֶהֲלוּ יָצָאנוּ מִמִּצְרַיִם, 'In haste we went out of Egypt.'

MAGGID

The broken matzah is lifted for all to see as the head of the household begins with the following brief explanation of the proceedings.

... we still look forward to a future redemption when we will celebrate Passover, as of old, in the Holy Temple in a rebuilt Jerusalem.

This is the bread of affliction that our fathers ate in the land of Egypt. Whoever is hungry — let him come and eat! Whoever is needy — let him come and celebrate Passover! Now, we are here; next year may we be in the Land of Israel! Now, we are slaves; next year may we be free men!

The Seder plate is removed and the second of the four cups of wine is poured. The youngest present asks the reasons for the unusual proceedings of the evening.

The Story[1] of the Exodus opens with a child's questions for Scripture often mentions this narrative in the form of a father's reply to his child's question.

The Four Questions note the contradictory observances of the Seder. We eat matzah and bitter herbs, which symbolize oppression and slavery ...

Why is this night different from all other nights?

1. **On all other nights** we may eat chametz and matzah, but on this night — only matzah.

2. **On all other nights** we eat many vegetables, but on this night — we eat maror.

25 □ THE FAMILY HAGGADAH

שֶׁבְּכָל הַלֵּילוֹת אֵין אָנוּ
מַטְבִּילִין אֲפִילוּ פַּעַם אֶחָת
הַלַּיְלָה הַזֶּה שְׁתֵּי פְעָמִים.
שֶׁבְּכָל הַלֵּילוֹת אָנוּ אוֹכְלִין בֵּין
יוֹשְׁבִין וּבֵין מְסֻבִּין הַלַּיְלָה הַזֶּה
כֻּלָּנוּ מְסֻבִּין:

The Seder plate is returned. The matzos are kept uncovered as
the Haggadah is recited in unison. The Haggadah should be translated,
if necessary, and the story of the Exodus should be amplified upon.

עֲבָדִים הָיִינוּ לְפַרְעֹה בְּמִצְרָיִם. וַיּוֹצִיאֵנוּ
יְהוה אֱלֹהֵינוּ מִשָּׁם בְּיָד חֲזָקָה
וּבִזְרֹעַ נְטוּיָה. וְאִלּוּ לֹא הוֹצִיא הַקָּדוֹשׁ בָּרוּךְ
הוּא אֶת אֲבוֹתֵינוּ מִמִּצְרַיִם הֲרֵי אָנוּ וּבָנֵינוּ וּבְנֵי
בָנֵינוּ מְשֻׁעְבָּדִים הָיִינוּ לְפַרְעֹה בְּמִצְרָיִם.
וַאֲפִילוּ כֻּלָּנוּ חֲכָמִים. כֻּלָּנוּ נְבוֹנִים. כֻּלָּנוּ זְקֵנִים.
כֻּלָּנוּ יוֹדְעִים אֶת הַתּוֹרָה. מִצְוָה עָלֵינוּ לְסַפֵּר
בִּיצִיאַת מִצְרָיִם. וְכָל הַמַּרְבֶּה לְסַפֵּר בִּיצִיאַת
מִצְרַיִם הֲרֵי זֶה מְשֻׁבָּח:

מַעֲשֶׂה בְּרַבִּי אֱלִיעֶזֶר וְרַבִּי יְהוֹשֻׁעַ וְרַבִּי
אֶלְעָזָר בֶּן עֲזַרְיָה וְרַבִּי עֲקִיבָא
וְרַבִּי טַרְפוֹן שֶׁהָיוּ מְסֻבִּין בִּבְנֵי בְרַק וְהָיוּ
מְסַפְּרִים בִּיצִיאַת מִצְרַיִם כָּל אוֹתוֹ הַלַּיְלָה עַד
שֶׁבָּאוּ תַלְמִידֵיהֶם וְאָמְרוּ לָהֶם. רַבּוֹתֵינוּ הִגִּיעַ
זְמַן קְרִיאַת שְׁמַע שֶׁל שַׁחֲרִית:

אָמַר רַבִּי אֶלְעָזָר בֶּן עֲזַרְיָה. הֲרֵי אֲנִי כְּבֶן
שִׁבְעִים שָׁנָה. וְלֹא זָכִיתִי שֶׁתֵּאָמֵר

3. On all other nights we do not dip even once, but on this night — twice.

but, at the same time we dip our vegetables and recline on couches, which indicate opulence and freedom!

4. On all other nights we eat either sitting or reclining, but on this night — we all recline.

The Seder plate is returned. The matzos are kept uncovered as the Haggadah is recited in unison. The Haggadah should be translated, if necessary, and the story of the Exodus should be amplified upon.

We were slaves to Pharaoh in Egypt, but HASHEM our God took us out from there with a mighty hand and an outstretched arm. Had not the Holy One, Blessed is He, taken our fathers out from Egypt, then we, our children, and our children's children would have remained enslaved to Pharaoh in Egypt. Even if we were all men of wisdom, understanding, experience, and knowledge of the Torah, it would still be an obligation upon us to tell about the Exodus from Egypt. The more one tells about the Exodus, the more he is praiseworthy.

The child is first given a brief summary of the entire epoch. — "We were slaves, and then God freed us." Subsequently, more and more details will be added to the narrative.

It happened that Rabbi Eliezer, Rabbi Yehoshua, Rabbi Elazar ben Azaryah, Rabbi Akiva, and Rabbi Tarfon were reclining (at the Seder) in Bnei Brak. They discussed the Exodus all that night until their students came and said to them: 'Our teachers, it is [daybreak] time for the reading of the morning Shema.'

Even great sages, who surely know the story, must recount it at great length.

Rabbi Elazar ben Azaryah said: I am like a seventy year old man, but I could not succeed in having the

27 ☐ THE FAMILY HAGGADAH

יְצִיאַת מִצְרַיִם בַּלֵּילוֹת. עַד שֶׁדְּרָשָׁהּ בֶּן זוֹמָא. שֶׁנֶּאֱמַר לְמַעַן תִּזְכֹּר אֶת יוֹם צֵאתְךָ מֵאֶרֶץ מִצְרַיִם כֹּל יְמֵי חַיֶּיךָ. יְמֵי חַיֶּיךָ הַיָּמִים. כֹּל יְמֵי חַיֶּיךָ הַלֵּילוֹת. וַחֲכָמִים אוֹמְרִים. יְמֵי חַיֶּיךָ הָעוֹלָם הַזֶּה. כֹּל יְמֵי חַיֶּיךָ לְהָבִיא לִימוֹת הַמָּשִׁיחַ:

בָּרוּךְ הַמָּקוֹם. בָּרוּךְ הוּא. בָּרוּךְ שֶׁנָּתַן תּוֹרָה לְעַמּוֹ יִשְׂרָאֵל. בָּרוּךְ הוּא. כְּנֶגֶד אַרְבָּעָה בָנִים דִּבְּרָה תוֹרָה. אֶחָד **חָכָם.** וְאֶחָד **רָשָׁע.** וְאֶחָד **תָּם.** וְאֶחָד **שֶׁאֵינוֹ יוֹדֵעַ** לִשְׁאוֹל:

חָכָם מָה הוּא אוֹמֵר. מָה הָעֵדֹת וְהַחֻקִּים וְהַמִּשְׁפָּטִים אֲשֶׁר צִוָּה יְהוָה אֱלֹהֵינוּ אֶתְכֶם. וְאַף אַתָּה אֱמָר לוֹ כְּהִלְכוֹת הַפֶּסַח. אֵין מַפְטִירִין אַחַר הַפֶּסַח אֲפִיקוֹמָן:

רָשָׁע מָה הוּא אוֹמֵר. מָה הָעֲבֹדָה הַזֹּאת לָכֶם. לָכֶם וְלֹא לוֹ. וּלְפִי שֶׁהוֹצִיא אֶת עַצְמוֹ מִן הַכְּלָל כָּפַר בְּעִקָּר. וְאַף אַתָּה הַקְהֵה אֶת שִׁנָּיו וֶאֱמָר לוֹ בַּעֲבוּר זֶה עָשָׂה יְהוָה לִי בְּצֵאתִי מִמִּצְרָיִם. לִי וְלֹא לוֹ. אִלּוּ הָיָה שָׁם לֹא הָיָה נִגְאָל:

תָּם מָה הוּא אוֹמֵר. מַה זֹּאת. וְאָמַרְתָּ אֵלָיו בְּחֹזֶק יָד הוֹצִיאָנוּ יְהוָה מִמִּצְרַיִם מִבֵּית עֲבָדִים:

וְשֶׁאֵינוֹ יוֹדֵעַ לִשְׁאוֹל אַתְּ פְּתַח לוֹ. שֶׁנֶּאֱמַר וְהִגַּדְתָּ לְבִנְךָ בַּיּוֹם הַהוּא לֵאמֹר בַּעֲבוּר זֶה עָשָׂה יְהוָה לִי בְּצֵאתִי מִמִּצְרָיִם:

KADDESH
URECHATZ
KARPAS
YACHATZ
MAGGID
RACHTZAH
MOTZI
MATZAH
MAROR
KORECH
SHULCHAN ORECH
TZAFUN
BARECH
HALLEL
NIRTZAH

Exodus from Egypt mentioned every night, until Ben Zoma expounded it: 'In order that you may remember the day you left Egypt all the days of your life' (Deuteronomy 16:3). The phrase 'the days of your life' would have indicated only the days; the addition of the word 'all,' includes the nights as well. But the Sages declare that 'the days of your life' would mean only the present world; the addition of 'all' includes the era of the Messiah.

One of the participants in the Bnei Brak Seder, Rabbi Elazar ben Azaryah, had a novel teaching about the requirement to remember the Exodus.

B lessed is the Omnipresent; blessed is He. Blessed is the One Who has given the Torah to His people Israel; blessed is He. Concerning four sons does the Torah speak: a **wise** one, a **wicked** one, a **simple** one, and one **who is unable to ask.**

From the various shades of expression in Scripture's description of the father-son dialogue, four types of offspring can be discerned.

T he **wise son** — what does he say? 'What are the testimonies, decrees, and ordinances which HASHEM, our God, has commanded you?' (Deuteronomy 6:20). Therefore explain to him the laws of the Passover offering: that one may not eat dessert after the final taste of the Passover offering.

The wise son seeks knowledge.

T he **wicked son** — what does he say? 'Of what purpose is this work to you?' (Exodus 12:26). He says, 'To you', thereby excluding himself. By excluding himself from the community of believers, he denies the basic principle of Judaism. Therefore, blunt his teeth and tell him: 'It is because of this that HASHEM did so for me when I went out of Egypt' (Exodus 13:8). 'For me,' but not for him — had he been there, he would not have been redeemed.

The wicked son looks down on the beliefs of his people and scoffs.

T he **simple son** — what does he say? 'What is this?' Tell him: 'With a strong hand did HASHEM take us out of Egypt, from the house of bondage' (Exodus 13:14).

The simple son asks a simple question.

A s for **the son who is unable to ask**, you must initiate the subject for him, as it is stated (Exodus 13:8): You shall tell your son on that day: 'It is because of this that HASHEM did so for me when I went out of Egypt.'

If the child does not ask, the parent must teach.

29 □ THE FAMILY HAGGADAH

יָכוֹל מֵרֹאשׁ חֹדֶשׁ. תַּלְמוּד לוֹמַר בַּיּוֹם הַהוּא. אִי בַּיּוֹם הַהוּא יָכוֹל מִבְּעוֹד יוֹם. תַּלְמוּד לוֹמַר בַּעֲבוּר זֶה. בַּעֲבוּר זֶה לֹא אָמַרְתִּי אֶלָּא בְּשָׁעָה שֶׁיֵּשׁ מַצָּה וּמָרוֹר מֻנָּחִים לְפָנֶיךָ:

מִתְּחִלָּה עוֹבְדֵי עֲבוֹדָה זָרָה הָיוּ אֲבוֹתֵינוּ. וְעַכְשָׁו קֵרְבָנוּ הַמָּקוֹם לַעֲבוֹדָתוֹ. שֶׁנֶּאֱמַר וַיֹּאמֶר יְהוֹשֻׁעַ אֶל כָּל הָעָם כֹּה אָמַר יהוה אֱלֹהֵי יִשְׂרָאֵל בְּעֵבֶר הַנָּהָר יָשְׁבוּ אֲבוֹתֵיכֶם מֵעוֹלָם תֶּרַח אֲבִי אַבְרָהָם וַאֲבִי נָחוֹר וַיַּעַבְדוּ אֱלֹהִים אֲחֵרִים: וָאֶקַּח אֶת אֲבִיכֶם אֶת אַבְרָהָם מֵעֵבֶר הַנָּהָר וָאוֹלֵךְ אוֹתוֹ בְּכָל אֶרֶץ כְּנָעַן וָאַרְבֶּה אֶת זַרְעוֹ וָאֶתֶּן לוֹ אֶת יִצְחָק: וָאֶתֵּן לְיִצְחָק אֶת יַעֲקֹב וְאֶת עֵשָׂו וָאֶתֵּן לְעֵשָׂו אֶת הַר שֵׂעִיר לָרֶשֶׁת אוֹתוֹ וְיַעֲקֹב וּבָנָיו יָרְדוּ מִצְרָיִם:

בָּרוּךְ שׁוֹמֵר הַבְטָחָתוֹ לְיִשְׂרָאֵל. בָּרוּךְ הוּא. שֶׁהַקָּדוֹשׁ בָּרוּךְ הוּא חִשַּׁב אֶת הַקֵּץ לַעֲשׂוֹת כְּמָה שֶׁאָמַר לְאַבְרָהָם אָבִינוּ בִּבְרִית בֵּין הַבְּתָרִים. שֶׁנֶּאֱמַר וַיֹּאמֶר לְאַבְרָם יָדֹעַ תֵּדַע כִּי גֵר יִהְיֶה זַרְעֲךָ בְּאֶרֶץ לֹא לָהֶם וַעֲבָדוּם וְעִנּוּ אֹתָם אַרְבַּע מֵאוֹת שָׁנָה: וְגַם אֶת הַגּוֹי אֲשֶׁר יַעֲבֹדוּ דָּן אָנֹכִי וְאַחֲרֵי כֵן יֵצְאוּ בִּרְכֻשׁ גָּדוֹל:

The matzos are covered and the cups lifted as the following paragraph is proclaimed joyously. On its conclusion, the cups are put down and the matzos are uncovered.

וְהִיא שֶׁעָמְדָה לַאֲבוֹתֵינוּ וְלָנוּ. שֶׁלֹּא אֶחָד בִּלְבַד עָמַד עָלֵינוּ לְכַלּוֹתֵנוּ. אֶלָּא שֶׁבְּכָל דּוֹר וָדוֹר עוֹמְדִים עָלֵינוּ לְכַלּוֹתֵנוּ. וְהַקָּדוֹשׁ בָּרוּךְ הוּא מַצִּילֵנוּ מִיָּדָם:

קַדֵּשׁ
KADDESH

וּרְחַץ
URECHATZ

כַּרְפַּס
KARPAS

יַחַץ
YACHATZ

מַגִּיד
MAGGID

רָחְצָה
RACHTZAH

מוֹצִיא
MOTZI

מַצָּה
MATZAH

מָרוֹר
MAROR

כּוֹרֵךְ
KORECH

שֻׁלְחָן עוֹרֵךְ
SHULCHAN ORECH

צָפוּן
TZAFUN

בָּרֵךְ
BARECH

הַלֵּל
HALLEL

נִרְצָה
NIRTZAH

God instructed Moses on the first of Nissan to prepare the nation for its imminent departure from Egypt.

One might think that the obligation to discuss the Exodus commences with the first day of the month of Nissan, but the Torah says: 'You shall tell your son on that day.' But the expression 'on that day' could be understood to mean only during the daytime; therefore the Torah adds: 'It is because of this that HASHEM did so for me when I went out of Egypt.' The pronoun 'this' implies something tangible, thus 'You shall tell your son' applies only when matzah and maror lie before you — at the Seder.

The spiritual greatness of our lofty Abrahamitic heritage is contrasted with the moral decay of our earliest ancestors.

Originally our ancestors were idol worshipers, but now the Omnipresent has brought us near to His service, as it is written (Joshua 24:2-4): Joshua said to all the people, 'So says HASHEM, God of Israel: Your fathers always lived beyond the Euphrates River, Terach the father of Abraham and Nachor, and they served other gods. Then I took your father Abraham from beyond the river and led him through all the land of Canaan. I multiplied his offspring and gave him Isaac. To Isaac I gave Jacob and Esau; to Esau I gave Mount Seir to inherit, but Jacob and his children went down to Egypt.'

Despite Israel's descent to Egypt, God's promise to Abraham was not forgotten.

Blessed is He Who keeps His pledge to Israel; blessed is He! For the Holy One, Blessed is He, calculated the end of the bondage in order to do as He said to our father Abraham at the Covenant between the Parts, as it is stated (Genesis 15:13-14): He said to Abram, 'Know with certainty that your offspring will be aliens in a land not their own, they will serve them and they will oppress them four hundred years; but also upon the nation which they shall serve will I execute judgment, and afterwards they shall leave with great possessions.'

The matzos are covered and the cups lifted as the following paragraph is proclaimed joyously. On its conclusion, the cups are put down and the matzos are uncovered.

Indeed, that promise has stood by us in all generations, through countless persecutions.

It is this that has stood by our fathers and us. For not only one has risen against us to annihilate us, but in every generation they rise against us to annihilate us. But the Holy One, Blessed is He, rescues us from their hand.

צֵא וּלְמַד. מַה בִּקֵּשׁ לָבָן הָאֲרַמִּי לַעֲשׂוֹת לְיַעֲקֹב אָבִינוּ. שֶׁפַּרְעֹה לֹא גָזַר אֶלָּא עַל הַזְּכָרִים וְלָבָן בִּקֵּשׁ לַעֲקוֹר אֶת הַכֹּל. שֶׁנֶּאֱמַר

אֲרַמִּי אֹבֵד אָבִי וַיֵּרֶד מִצְרַיְמָה וַיָּגָר שָׁם בִּמְתֵי מְעָט וַיְהִי שָׁם לְגוֹי גָּדוֹל עָצוּם וָרָב:

וַיֵּרֶד מִצְרַיְמָה. אָנוּס עַל פִּי הַדִּבּוּר:

וַיָּגָר שָׁם. מְלַמֵּד שֶׁלֹּא יָרַד יַעֲקֹב אָבִינוּ לְהִשְׁתַּקֵּעַ בְּמִצְרַיִם אֶלָּא לָגוּר שָׁם. שֶׁנֶּאֱמַר וַיֹּאמְרוּ אֶל פַּרְעֹה לָגוּר בָּאָרֶץ בָּאנוּ כִּי אֵין מִרְעֶה לַצֹּאן אֲשֶׁר לַעֲבָדֶיךָ כִּי כָבֵד הָרָעָב בְּאֶרֶץ כְּנָעַן וְעַתָּה יֵשְׁבוּ נָא עֲבָדֶיךָ בְּאֶרֶץ גֹּשֶׁן:

בִּמְתֵי מְעָט. כְּמָה שֶׁנֶּאֱמַר בְּשִׁבְעִים נֶפֶשׁ יָרְדוּ אֲבֹתֶיךָ מִצְרַיְמָה וְעַתָּה שָׂמְךָ יְהוָה אֱלֹהֶיךָ כְּכוֹכְבֵי הַשָּׁמַיִם לָרֹב:

וַיְהִי שָׁם לְגוֹי. מְלַמֵּד שֶׁהָיוּ יִשְׂרָאֵל מְצֻיָּנִים שָׁם:

גָּדוֹל עָצוּם. כְּמָה שֶׁנֶּאֱמַר וּבְנֵי יִשְׂרָאֵל פָּרוּ וַיִּשְׁרְצוּ וַיִּרְבּוּ וַיַּעַצְמוּ בִּמְאֹד מְאֹד וַתִּמָּלֵא הָאָרֶץ אֹתָם:

וָרָב. כְּמָה שֶׁנֶּאֱמַר רְבָבָה כְּצֶמַח הַשָּׂדֶה נְתַתִּיךְ וַתִּרְבִּי וַתִּגְדְּלִי וַתָּבֹאִי בַּעֲדִי עֲדָיִים שָׁדַיִם נָכֹנוּ וּשְׂעָרֵךְ צִמֵּחַ וְאַתְּ עֵרֹם וְעֶרְיָה: וָאֶעֱבֹר עָלַיִךְ וָאֶרְאֵךְ מִתְבּוֹסֶסֶת בְּדָמָיִךְ וָאֹמַר לָךְ בְּדָמַיִךְ חֲיִי וָאֹמַר לָךְ בְּדָמַיִךְ חֲיִי:

וַיָּרֵעוּ אֹתָנוּ הַמִּצְרִים וַיְעַנּוּנוּ וַיִּתְּנוּ עָלֵינוּ עֲבֹדָה קָשָׁה:

וַיָּרֵעוּ אֹתָנוּ הַמִּצְרִים. כְּמָה שֶׁנֶּאֱמַר הָבָה נִתְחַכְּמָה לוֹ פֶּן יִרְבֶּה וְהָיָה כִּי תִקְרֶאנָה

קַדֵּשׁ
KADDESH

וּרְחַץ
URECHATZ

כַּרְפַּס
KARPAS

יַחַץ
YACHATZ

מַגִּיד
MAGGID

רָחְצָה
RACHTZAH

מוֹצִיא
MOTZI

מַצָּה
MATZAH

מָרוֹר
MAROR

כּוֹרֵךְ
KORECH

שֻׁלְחָן
עוֹרֵךְ
SHULCHAN
ORECH

צָפוּן
TZAFUN

בָּרֵךְ
BARECH

הַלֵּל
HALLEL

נִרְצָה
NIRTZAH

Even before the Exodus, that promise protected us from Laban, whose evil was, in a sense, more potent that Pharoah's.

Details of Israel's descent, oppression, prayers, and deliverance are now added in a word-by-word exposition of four verses in Deuteronomy. The first verse speaks of the descent to Egypt.

Our ancestors' descent was part of the Divine plan.

They thought their stay would be short.

They were few in number ...

but remained distinctive ...

powerful ...

and numerous.

Go and learn what Laban the Aramean attempted to do to our father Jacob! For Pharaoh decreed only against the males, Laban attempted to uproot everything, as it is said (Deuteronomy 26:5):

An Aramean attempted to destroy my father. Then he descended to Egypt and sojourned there, with few people; and there he became a nation — great, mighty, and numerous.

Then he descended to Egypt — compelled by Divine decree.

He sojourned there — this teaches that our father Jacob did not descend to Egypt to settle, but only to sojourn temporarily, as it says (Genesis 47:4): They (the sons of Jacob) said to Pharaoh: 'We have come to sojourn in this land because there is no pasture for the flocks of your servants, because the famine is severe in the land of Canaan. And now, please let your servants dwell in the land of Goshen.'

With few people — as it is written (Deuteronomy 10:22): With seventy persons, your forefathers descended to Egypt, and now HASHEM, your God, has made you as numerous as the stars of heaven.

There he became a nation — this teaches that the Israelites were distinctive there.

Great, mighty — as it says (Exodus 1:7): And the children of Israel were fruitful, increased greatly, multiplied, and became very, very mighty; and the land was filled with them.

Numerous — as it says (Ezekiel 16:7,6): I made you as numerous as the plants of the field; you grew and developed, and became charming, beautiful of figure; your hair grown long; but, you were naked and bare. And I passed over you and saw you downtrodden in your blood and I said to you: 'Through your blood shall you live!' And I said to you: 'Through your blood shall you live!'.

The second verse describes the oppressiveness of the Egyptians.

Subtly, with guile, the Egyptians laid their plans.

The Egyptians did evil to us and afflicted us; and imposed hard labor upon us (Deuteronomy 26:6).

The Egyptians did evil to us — as it says (Exodus 1:10): Let us deal with them wisely lest they multiply and, if we happen to be at war, they may join our

33 □ THE FAMILY HAGGADAH

מִלְחָמָה וְנוֹסַף גַּם הוּא עַל שׂנְאֵינוּ וְנִלְחַם בָּנוּ וְעָלָה מִן הָאָרֶץ:

וַיְעַנּוּנוּ. כְּמָה שֶׁנֶּאֱמַר וַיָּשִׂימוּ עָלָיו שָׂרֵי מִסִּים לְמַעַן עַנֹּתוֹ בְּסִבְלֹתָם וַיִּבֶן עָרֵי מִסְכְּנוֹת לְפַרְעֹה אֶת פִּתֹם וְאֶת רַעַמְסֵס:

וַיִּתְּנוּ עָלֵינוּ עֲבֹדָה קָשָׁה. כְּמָה שֶׁנֶּאֱמַר וַיַּעֲבִדוּ מִצְרַיִם אֶת בְּנֵי יִשְׂרָאֵל בְּפָרֶךְ:

וַנִּצְעַק אֶל יהוה אֱלֹהֵי אֲבֹתֵינוּ וַיִּשְׁמַע יהוה אֶת קֹלֵנוּ וַיַּרְא אֶת עָנְיֵנוּ וְאֶת עֲמָלֵנוּ וְאֶת לַחֲצֵנוּ:

וַנִּצְעַק אֶל יהוה אֱלֹהֵי אֲבֹתֵינוּ כְּמָה שֶׁנֶּאֱמַר וַיְהִי בַיָּמִים הָרַבִּים הָהֵם וַיָּמָת מֶלֶךְ מִצְרַיִם וַיֵּאָנְחוּ בְנֵי יִשְׂרָאֵל מִן הָעֲבֹדָה וַיִּזְעָקוּ וַתַּעַל שַׁוְעָתָם אֶל הָאֱלֹהִים מִן הָעֲבֹדָה:

וַיִּשְׁמַע יהוה אֶת קֹלֵנוּ. כְּמָה שֶׁנֶּאֱמַר וַיִּשְׁמַע אֱלֹהִים אֶת נַאֲקָתָם וַיִּזְכֹּר אֱלֹהִים אֶת בְּרִיתוֹ אֶת אַבְרָהָם אֶת יִצְחָק וְאֶת יַעֲקֹב:

וַיַּרְא אֶת עָנְיֵנוּ. זוֹ פְּרִישׁוּת דֶּרֶךְ אֶרֶץ. כְּמָה שֶׁנֶּאֱמַר וַיַּרְא אֱלֹהִים אֶת בְּנֵי יִשְׂרָאֵל וַיֵּדַע אֱלֹהִים:

וְאֶת עֲמָלֵנוּ. אֵלּוּ הַבָּנִים. כְּמָה שֶׁנֶּאֱמַר כָּל הַבֵּן הַיִּלּוֹד הַיְאֹרָה תַּשְׁלִיכֻהוּ וְכָל הַבַּת תְּחַיּוּן:

וְאֶת לַחֲצֵנוּ. זוֹ הַדְּחַק. כְּמָה שֶׁנֶּאֱמַר וְגַם רָאִיתִי אֶת הַלַּחַץ אֲשֶׁר מִצְרַיִם לֹחֲצִים אֹתָם:

וַיּוֹצִאֵנוּ יהוה מִמִּצְרַיִם בְּיָד חֲזָקָה וּבִזְרֹעַ נְטוּיָה וּבְמֹרָא גָּדֹל וּבְאֹתוֹת וּבְמֹפְתִים:

וַיּוֹצִאֵנוּ יהוה מִמִּצְרַיִם. לֹא עַל יְדֵי מַלְאָךְ

34 □ הגדה של פסח

enemies and fight against us and then leave the country.

They forced work upon us ...

And Afflicted us — as it says (Exodus 1:11): They set taskmasters over them in order to oppress them with their burdens; and they built Pithom and Raamses as treasure cities for Pharaoh.

back-breaking labor.

They imposed hard labor upon us — as it says (Exodus 1:13): The Egyptians subjugated the children of Israel with hard labor.

The third verse speaks of our prayers and God's response.

We cried out to HASHEM, the God of our fathers; and HASHEM heard our cry and saw our affliction, our burden, and our oppression (Deuteronomy 26:7).

When the slave labor imposed upon us became unbearable, we cried to God.

We cried out to HASHEM, the God of our fathers — as it says (Exodus 2:23): It happened in the course of those many days that the king of Egypt died; and the children of Israel groaned because of the servitude and cried; their cry because of the servitude rose up to God.'

He listened and recalled His covenant with our forebears.

HASHEM heard our cry — as it says (Exodus 2:24): God heard their groaning, and God recalled His covenant with Abraham, with Isaac, and with Jacob.

He saw how our families were disrupted ...

And saw our affliction — that is the disruption of family life, as it says (Exodus 2:25): God saw the children of Israel and God took note.

how our children were killed ...

Our burden — refers to the children as it says (Exodus 1:22): Every son that is born you shall cast into the river, but every daughter you shall let live.

and how we suffered oppression.

Our oppression — refers to the pressure expressed in the words (Exodus 3:9): I have also seen how the Egyptians are oppressing them.

The fourth verse tells of the deliverance.

HASHEM brought us out of Egypt with a mighty hand and with an outstretched arm, with great awe, with signs and with wonders (Deuteronomy 26:8).

HASHEM brought us out of Egypt — not through an

35 ☐ THE FAMILY HAGGADAH

וְלֹא עַל יְדֵי שָׂרָף וְלֹא עַל יְדֵי שָׁלִיחַ. אֶלָּא
הַקָּדוֹשׁ בָּרוּךְ הוּא בִּכְבוֹדוֹ וּבְעַצְמוֹ. שֶׁנֶּאֱמַר
וְעָבַרְתִּי בְאֶרֶץ מִצְרַיִם בַּלַּיְלָה הַזֶּה וְהִכֵּיתִי כָל
בְּכוֹר בְּאֶרֶץ מִצְרַיִם מֵאָדָם וְעַד בְּהֵמָה וּבְכָל
אֱלֹהֵי מִצְרַיִם אֶעֱשֶׂה שְׁפָטִים אֲנִי יהוה:

וְעָבַרְתִּי בְאֶרֶץ מִצְרַיִם בַּלַּיְלָה הַזֶּה. אֲנִי וְלֹא
מַלְאָךְ. וְהִכֵּיתִי כָל בְּכוֹר בְּאֶרֶץ מִצְרָיִם. אֲנִי
וְלֹא שָׂרָף. וּבְכָל אֱלֹהֵי מִצְרַיִם אֶעֱשֶׂה שְׁפָטִים.
אֲנִי וְלֹא הַשָּׁלִיחַ. אֲנִי יהוה. אֲנִי הוּא וְלֹא אַחֵר:

בְּיָד חֲזָקָה. זוֹ הַדֶּבֶר. כְּמָה שֶׁנֶּאֱמַר הִנֵּה יַד
יהוה הוֹיָה בְּמִקְנְךָ אֲשֶׁר בַּשָּׂדֶה בַּסּוּסִים
בַּחֲמֹרִים בַּגְּמַלִּים בַּבָּקָר וּבַצֹּאן דֶּבֶר כָּבֵד מְאֹד:

וּבִזְרֹעַ נְטוּיָה. זוֹ הַחֶרֶב. כְּמָה שֶׁנֶּאֱמַר
וְחַרְבּוֹ שְׁלוּפָה בְּיָדוֹ נְטוּיָה עַל יְרוּשָׁלָיִם:

וּבְמֹרָא גָדֹל. זוֹ גִּלּוּי שְׁכִינָה. כְּמָה שֶׁנֶּאֱמַר
אוֹ הֲנִסָּה אֱלֹהִים לָבוֹא לָקַחַת לוֹ גוֹי מִקֶּרֶב גּוֹי
בְּמַסֹּת בְּאֹתֹת וּבְמוֹפְתִים וּבְמִלְחָמָה וּבְיָד
חֲזָקָה וּבִזְרוֹעַ נְטוּיָה וּבְמוֹרָאִים גְּדֹלִים כְּכֹל
אֲשֶׁר עָשָׂה לָכֶם יהוה אֱלֹהֵיכֶם בְּמִצְרַיִם
לְעֵינֶיךָ:

וּבְאֹתוֹת זֶה הַמַּטֶּה. כְּמָה שֶׁנֶּאֱמַר וְאֶת
הַמַּטֶּה הַזֶּה תִּקַּח בְּיָדֶךָ אֲשֶׁר תַּעֲשֶׂה בּוֹ אֶת
הָאֹתֹת:

וּבְמֹפְתִים זֶה הַדָּם. כְּמָה שֶׁנֶּאֱמַר וְנָתַתִּי
מוֹפְתִים בַּשָּׁמַיִם וּבָאָרֶץ

As each of the words דָּם, blood, אֵשׁ, fire, and עָשָׁן, smoke, is said, a bit of wine is removed from the cup, with the finger or by pouring.

דָּם וָאֵשׁ וְתִמְרוֹת עָשָׁן:
דָּבָר אַחֵר בְּיָד חֲזָקָה שְׁתַּיִם. וּבִזְרֹעַ נְטוּיָה
שְׁתַּיִם. וּבְמֹרָא גָדֹל שְׁתַּיִם. וּבְאֹתוֹת שְׁתַּיִם.

No angel, no agent — only God, Himself, effected the redemption.

angel, not through a seraph, not through a messenger, but the Holy One, Blessed is He, in His glory, Himself, as it says (Exodus 12:12): I will pass through the land of Egypt on that night; I will slay all the firstborn in the land of Egypt from man to beast; and upon all the gods of Egypt will I execute judgments; I, HASHEM.

'I will pass through the land of Egypt on that night' — I and no angel; 'I will slay all the firstborn in the land of Egypt' — I and no seraph; 'And upon all the gods of Egypt will I execute judgments' — I and no messenger; 'I, HASHEM' — it is I and no other.

His hand smote the animals that the Egyptians had worshiped as gods

With a mighty hand — refers to the pestilence, as it says (Exodus 9:3): Behold, the hand of HASHEM shall strike your cattle which are in the field, the horses, the donkeys, the camels, the herds, and the flocks — a very severe pestilence.

... while His sword slew their firstborn.

With an outstretched arm — refers to the sword, as it says (I Chronicles 21:16): His drawn sword in his hand, outstretched over Jerusalem.

He revealed Himself by extracting the Israelites from among the Egyptians,

With great awe — alludes to the revelation of the Shechinah, as it says (Deuteronomy 4:34): Has God ever attempted to take unto Himself a nation from the midst of another nation by trials, miraculous signs, and wonders, by war and with a mighty hand and outstretched arm and by awesome revelations, as all that HASHEM your God did for you in Egypt, before your eyes?

and in the plagues invoked by Moses' staff ...

With signs — refers to the miracles performed with the staff as it says (Exodus 4:17): Take this staff in your hand, that you may perform the miraculous signs with it.

the first of which was Blood.

With wonders — alludes to the blood, as it says (Joel 3:3): I will show wonders in the heavens and on the earth:

As each of the words דָּם, blood, אֵשׁ, fire, and עָשָׁן, smoke, is said, a bit of wine is removed from the cup, with the finger or by pouring.

Blood, fire, and columns of smoke.

This verse also alludes to the other plagues.

Another explanation of the preceding verse: [Each phrase represents two plagues], hence: **mighty hand** — two; **outstretched arm** — two; **great awe** — two;

וּבְמוֹפְתִים שְׁתַּיִם: אֵלּוּ עֶשֶׂר מַכּוֹת שֶׁהֵבִיא הַקָּדוֹשׁ בָּרוּךְ הוּא עַל הַמִּצְרִים בְּמִצְרַיִם וְאֵלּוּ הֵן:

*As each of the Plagues is mentioned, a bit of wine is removed from the cup.
The same is done by each word of Rabbi Yehudah's mnemonic.*

דָּם. צְפַרְדֵּעַ. כִּנִּים. עָרוֹב. דֶּבֶר. שְׁחִין. בָּרָד. אַרְבֶּה. חֹשֶׁךְ. מַכַּת בְּכוֹרוֹת:

רַבִּי יְהוּדָה הָיָה נוֹתֵן בָּהֶם סִמָּנִים:

דְּצַ"ךְ עַדַ"שׁ בְּאַחַ"ב:

The cups are refilled. The wine that was removed is not used.

רַבִּי יוֹסֵי הַגְּלִילִי אוֹמֵר. מִנַּיִן אַתָּה אוֹמֵר שֶׁלָּקוּ הַמִּצְרִים בְּמִצְרַיִם עֶשֶׂר מַכּוֹת וְעַל הַיָּם לָקוּ חֲמִשִּׁים מַכּוֹת. בְּמִצְרַיִם מָה הוּא אוֹמֵר. וַיֹּאמְרוּ הַחַרְטֻמִּם אֶל פַּרְעֹה אֶצְבַּע אֱלֹהִים הִוא. וְעַל הַיָּם מָה הוּא אוֹמֵר. וַיַּרְא יִשְׂרָאֵל אֶת הַיָּד הַגְּדֹלָה אֲשֶׁר עָשָׂה יהוה בְּמִצְרַיִם וַיִּירְאוּ הָעָם אֶת יהוה וַיַּאֲמִינוּ בַּיהוה וּבְמֹשֶׁה עַבְדּוֹ. כַּמָּה לָקוּ בְאֶצְבַּע עֶשֶׂר מַכּוֹת. אֱמוֹר מֵעַתָּה בְּמִצְרַיִם לָקוּ עֶשֶׂר מַכּוֹת וְעַל הַיָּם לָקוּ חֲמִשִּׁים מַכּוֹת:

רַבִּי אֱלִיעֶזֶר אוֹמֵר. מִנַּיִן שֶׁכָּל מַכָּה וּמַכָּה שֶׁהֵבִיא הַקָּדוֹשׁ בָּרוּךְ הוּא עַל הַמִּצְרִים בְּמִצְרַיִם הָיְתָה שֶׁל אַרְבַּע מַכּוֹת. שֶׁנֶּאֱמַר יְשַׁלַּח בָּם חֲרוֹן אַפּוֹ עֶבְרָה וָזַעַם וְצָרָה מִשְׁלַחַת מַלְאֲכֵי רָעִים: עֶבְרָה אַחַת. וָזַעַם שְׁתַּיִם. וְצָרָה שָׁלֹשׁ. מִשְׁלַחַת מַלְאֲכֵי רָעִים אַרְבַּע: אֱמוֹר מֵעַתָּה בְּמִצְרַיִם לָקוּ אַרְבָּעִים מַכּוֹת וְעַל הַיָּם לָקוּ מָאתַיִם מַכּוֹת:

הַגָּדָה שֶׁל פֶּסַח

signs — two; **wonders** — two. These are the ten plagues which the Holy One, Blessed is He, brought upon the Egyptians in Egypt, namely:

As each of the Plagues is mentioned, a bit of wine is removed from the cup. The same is done by each word of Rabbi Yehudah's mnemonic.

Some wine is removed from the cup in compassion for the Egyptians. Although they oppressed us, we must not rejoice at the suffering of other humans.

1. Blood 2. Frogs 3. Vermin 4. Wild Beasts 5. Pestilence 6. Boils 7. Hail 8. Locusts 9. Darkness   10. Plague of the First-born.

Rabbi Judah abbreviated them by their Hebrew initials:

D'TZACH, ADASH, B'ACHAB

The cups are refilled. The wine that was removed is not used.

Rabbi Yose the Galilean said: How does one derive that the Egyptians were struck with ten plagues in Egypt, but with fifty plagues at the Sea? — Concerning the plagues in Egypt the Torah states (Exodus 8:15): The magicians said to Pharaoh, 'It is the finger of God.' However, of those at the Sea, the Torah relates (ibid. 14:31): Israel saw the great 'hand' which HASHEM laid upon the Egyptians, the people feared HASHEM and they believed in HASHEM and in His servant Moses. How many plagues did they receive with the finger? Ten! Then conclude that if they suffered ten plagues in Egypt [where they were struck with a finger], they must have been made to suffer fifty plagues at the Sea [where they were struck with a whole hand].

Scripture describes each of the Ten Plagues in detail, but all combined are but the flick of a finger compared to the blow delivered at the Sea of Reeds.

Rabbi Eliezer said: How does one derive that every plague that the Holy One, Blessed is He, inflicted upon the Egyptians in Egypt was equal to four plagues? — For it is written (Psalms 78:49): He sent upon them His fierce anger: wrath, fury, and trouble, a band of emissaries of evil. [Since each plague in Egypt consisted of] 1) wrath, 2) fury, 3) trouble and 4) a band of emissaries of evil, therefore conclude that in Egypt they were struck by forty plagues and at the Sea by two hundred!

Even the detailed account of each plague reveals but a fraction of its actual severity.

39 □ THE FAMILY HAGGADAH

רַבִּי עֲקִיבָא אוֹמֵר. מִנַּיִן שֶׁכָּל מַכָּה וּמַכָּה שֶׁהֵבִיא הַקָּדוֹשׁ בָּרוּךְ הוּא עַל הַמִּצְרִים בְּמִצְרַיִם הָיְתָה שֶׁל חָמֵשׁ מַכּוֹת. שֶׁנֶּאֱמַר יְשַׁלַּח בָּם חֲרוֹן אַפּוֹ עֶבְרָה וָזַעַם וְצָרָה מִשְׁלַחַת מַלְאֲכֵי רָעִים. חֲרוֹן אַפּוֹ אַחַת. עֶבְרָה שְׁתַּיִם. וָזַעַם שָׁלֹשׁ. וְצָרָה אַרְבַּע. מִשְׁלַחַת מַלְאֲכֵי רָעִים חָמֵשׁ: אֱמוֹר מֵעַתָּה בְּמִצְרַיִם לָקוּ חֲמִשִּׁים מַכּוֹת וְעַל הַיָּם לָקוּ חֲמִשִּׁים וּמָאתַיִם מַכּוֹת:

כַּמָּה מַעֲלוֹת טוֹבוֹת לַמָּקוֹם עָלֵינוּ:

אִלּוּ הוֹצִיאָנוּ מִמִּצְרַיִם

דַּיֵּנוּ: וְלֹא עָשָׂה בָהֶם שְׁפָטִים

אִלּוּ עָשָׂה בָהֶם שְׁפָטִים

דַּיֵּנוּ: וְלֹא עָשָׂה בֵאלֹהֵיהֶם

אִלּוּ עָשָׂה בֵאלֹהֵיהֶם

דַּיֵּנוּ: וְלֹא הָרַג אֶת בְּכוֹרֵיהֶם

אִלּוּ הָרַג אֶת בְּכוֹרֵיהֶם

דַּיֵּנוּ: וְלֹא נָתַן לָנוּ אֶת מָמוֹנָם

אִלּוּ נָתַן לָנוּ אֶת מָמוֹנָם

דַּיֵּנוּ: וְלֹא קָרַע לָנוּ אֶת הַיָּם

אִלּוּ קָרַע לָנוּ אֶת הַיָּם

דַּיֵּנוּ: וְלֹא הֶעֱבִירָנוּ בְּתוֹכוֹ בֶּחָרָבָה

אִלּוּ הֶעֱבִירָנוּ בְּתוֹכוֹ בֶּחָרָבָה

דַּיֵּנוּ: וְלֹא שִׁקַּע צָרֵינוּ בְּתוֹכוֹ

אִלּוּ שִׁקַּע צָרֵינוּ בְּתוֹכוֹ

וְלֹא סִפֵּק צָרְכֵּנוּ בַּמִּדְבָּר

אַרְבָּעִים שָׁנָה

דַּיֵּנוּ: אִלּוּ סִפֵּק צָרְכֵּנוּ בַּמִּדְבָּר אַרְבָּעִים שָׁנָה

דַּיֵּנוּ: וְלֹא הֶאֱכִילָנוּ אֶת הַמָּן

A deeper reading of the verses indicates that even more punishment was visited upon the Egyptians.

R abbi Akiva said: How does one derive that each plague that the Holy One, Blessed is He, inflicted upon the Egyptians in Egypt was equal to five plagues? — For it is written: He sent upon them His fierce anger, wrath, fury, trouble, and a band of emissaries of evil. [Since each plague in Egypt consisted of] 1) fierce anger, 2) wrath, 3) fury, 4) trouble, and 5) a band of emissaries of evil, therefore conclude that in Egypt they were struck by fifty plagues and at the sea by two hundred and fifty!

The Omnipresent has bestowed so many favors upon us!

In bringing us forth from slavery, God brought punishments upon our oppressors the Egyptians, their gods, their eldest, and their property ...

Had He brought us out of Egypt,
but not executed judgments against the Egyptians,
            it would have sufficed us.

Had He executed judgments against them,
but not upon their gods,   it would have sufficed us.

Had He executed judgments against their gods,
but not slain their firstborn,it would have sufficed us.

Had He slain their firstborn,
but not given us their wealth,it would have sufficed us.

Had He given us their wealth
but not split the Sea for us,it would have sufficed us.

He effected our physical salvation by leading us through the split Sea and catering to our bodily needs ...

Had He split the Sea for us,
but not led us through it on dry land,
            it would have sufficed us.

Had He led us through it on dry land,
but not drowned our oppressors in it,
            it would have sufficed us.

Had He drowned our oppressors in it,
but not provided for our needs in the desert
for forty years,   it would have sufficed us.

Had He provided for our needs in the desert
for forty years,
but not fed us the Manna, it would have sufficed us.

41 □ THE FAMILY HAGGADAH

אִלּוּ הֶאֱכִילָנוּ אֶת הַמָּן

וְלֹא נָתַן לָנוּ אֶת הַשַּׁבָּת   דַּיֵּנוּ:

אִלּוּ נָתַן לָנוּ אֶת הַשַּׁבָּת

וְלֹא קֵרְבָנוּ לִפְנֵי הַר סִינַי   דַּיֵּנוּ:

אִלּוּ קֵרְבָנוּ לִפְנֵי הַר סִינַי

וְלֹא נָתַן לָנוּ אֶת הַתּוֹרָה   דַּיֵּנוּ:

אִלּוּ נָתַן לָנוּ אֶת הַתּוֹרָה

וְלֹא הִכְנִיסָנוּ לְאֶרֶץ יִשְׂרָאֵל   דַּיֵּנוּ:

אִלּוּ הִכְנִיסָנוּ לְאֶרֶץ יִשְׂרָאֵל

וְלֹא בָנָה לָנוּ אֶת בֵּית הַבְּחִירָה   דַּיֵּנוּ:

עַל אַחַת כַּמָּה וְכַמָּה טוֹבָה כְפוּלָה וּמְכֻפֶּלֶת לַמָּקוֹם עָלֵינוּ. שֶׁהוֹצִיאָנוּ מִמִּצְרַיִם. וְעָשָׂה בָהֶם שְׁפָטִים. וְעָשָׂה בֵאלֹהֵיהֶם. וְהָרַג אֶת בְּכוֹרֵיהֶם. וְנָתַן לָנוּ אֶת מָמוֹנָם. וְקָרַע לָנוּ אֶת הַיָּם. וְהֶעֱבִירָנוּ בְתוֹכוֹ בֶּחָרָבָה. וְשִׁקַּע צָרֵינוּ בְתוֹכוֹ. וְסִפֵּק צָרְכֵּנוּ בַּמִּדְבָּר אַרְבָּעִים שָׁנָה. וְהֶאֱכִילָנוּ אֶת הַמָּן. וְנָתַן לָנוּ אֶת הַשַּׁבָּת. וְקֵרְבָנוּ לִפְנֵי הַר סִינַי. וְנָתַן לָנוּ אֶת הַתּוֹרָה. וְהִכְנִיסָנוּ לְאֶרֶץ יִשְׂרָאֵל. וּבָנָה לָנוּ אֶת בֵּית הַבְּחִירָה לְכַפֵּר עַל כָּל עֲוֹנוֹתֵינוּ:

רַבָּן גַּמְלִיאֵל הָיָה אוֹמֵר. כָּל שֶׁלֹּא אָמַר שְׁלֹשָׁה דְּבָרִים אֵלּוּ בַּפֶּסַח לֹא יָצָא יְדֵי חוֹבָתוֹ. וְאֵלּוּ הֵן.

פֶּסַח   מַצָּה   וּמָרוֹר

פֶּסַח שֶׁהָיוּ אֲבוֹתֵינוּ אוֹכְלִים בִּזְמַן שֶׁבֵּית הַמִּקְדָּשׁ הָיָה קַיָּם עַל שׁוּם מָה. עַל שׁוּם שֶׁפָּסַח הַקָּדוֹשׁ בָּרוּךְ הוּא עַל בָּתֵּי אֲבוֹתֵינוּ בְמִצְרַיִם. שֶׁנֶּאֱמַר וַאֲמַרְתֶּם זֶבַח פֶּסַח

and He presented us with spiritual redemption in the form of the Sabbath, the Torah, the Holy Land and the Temple.

Had He fed us the Manna,
but not given us the Sabbath, it would have sufficed us.

Had He given us the Sabbath,
but not brought us before Mount Sinai,
it would have sufficed us.

Had He brought us before Mount Sinai,
but not given us the Torah, it would have sufficed us.

Had He given us the Torah,
but not brought us into the Land of Israel,
it would have sufficed us.

Had He brought us into the Land of Israel,
but not built the Temple for us,
it would have sufficed us.

Had God blessed us with even one of these fifteen gifts, it would have been enough to make us immeasurably grateful. How much more must we express our gratitude for all of them.

Thus, how much more so, should we be grateful to the Omnipresent for all the numerous favors He showered upon us: He brought us out of Egypt; executed judgments against the Egyptians; and against their gods; slew their firstborn; gave us their wealth; split the Sea for us; led us through it on dry land; drowned our oppressors in it; provided for our needs in the desert for forty years; fed us the Manna; gave us the Sabbath; brought us before Mount Sinai; gave us the Torah; brought us to the Land of Israel; and built us the Temple to atone for all our sins.

But before singing His praise, we must mention the commandments of this night, and elaborate on their significance.

Rabban Gamliel used to say: Whoever has not explained the following three things on Passover has not fulfilled his duty, namely: **Pesach** — the Passover Offering; **Matzah** — the Unleavened Bread; **Maror** — the Bitter Herbs.

The Pesach (Passover offering) recalls God's personal intervention on our behalf.

Pesach — Why did our fathers eat a Passover offering during the period when the Temple still stood? — Because the Holy One, Blessed is He, passed over the houses of our fathers in Egypt, as it is written (Exodus 12:27): You shall say: 'It is a Passover

43 □ THE FAMILY HAGGADAH

הוּא לַיהוה אֲשֶׁר פָּסַח עַל בָּתֵּי בְנֵי יִשְׂרָאֵל בְּמִצְרַיִם בְּנָגְפּוֹ אֶת מִצְרַיִם וְאֶת בָּתֵּינוּ הִצִּיל וַיִּקֹּד הָעָם וַיִּשְׁתַּחֲווּ:

The middle matzah is lifted and displayed while the following paragraph is recited.

מַצָּה זוֹ שֶׁאָנוּ אוֹכְלִים עַל שׁוּם מָה. עַל שׁוּם שֶׁלֹּא הִסְפִּיק בְּצֵקָם שֶׁל אֲבוֹתֵינוּ לְהַחֲמִיץ עַד שֶׁנִּגְלָה עֲלֵיהֶם מֶלֶךְ מַלְכֵי הַמְּלָכִים הַקָּדוֹשׁ בָּרוּךְ הוּא וּגְאָלָם. שֶׁנֶּאֱמַר וַיֹּאפוּ אֶת הַבָּצֵק אֲשֶׁר הוֹצִיאוּ מִמִּצְרַיִם עֻגֹת מַצּוֹת כִּי לֹא חָמֵץ כִּי גֹרְשׁוּ מִמִּצְרַיִם וְלֹא יָכְלוּ לְהִתְמַהְמֵהַּ וְגַם צֵדָה לֹא עָשׂוּ לָהֶם:

The maror is lifted and displayed while the following paragraph is recited.

מָרוֹר זֶה שֶׁאָנוּ אוֹכְלִים עַל שׁוּם מָה. עַל שׁוּם שֶׁמֵּרְרוּ הַמִּצְרִים אֶת חַיֵּי אֲבוֹתֵינוּ בְּמִצְרָיִם. שֶׁנֶּאֱמַר וַיְמָרְרוּ אֶת חַיֵּיהֶם בַּעֲבֹדָה קָשָׁה בְּחֹמֶר וּבִלְבֵנִים וּבְכָל עֲבֹדָה בַּשָּׂדֶה אֵת כָּל עֲבֹדָתָם אֲשֶׁר עָבְדוּ בָהֶם בְּפָרֶךְ:

בְּכָל דּוֹר וָדוֹר חַיָּב אָדָם לִרְאוֹת אֶת עַצְמוֹ כְּאִלּוּ הוּא יָצָא מִמִּצְרַיִם. שֶׁנֶּאֱמַר וְהִגַּדְתָּ לְבִנְךָ בַּיּוֹם הַהוּא לֵאמֹר בַּעֲבוּר זֶה עָשָׂה יהוה לִי בְּצֵאתִי מִמִּצְרָיִם. לֹא אֶת אֲבוֹתֵינוּ בִּלְבָד גָּאַל הַקָּדוֹשׁ בָּרוּךְ הוּא אֶלָּא אַף אֹתָנוּ גָּאַל עִמָּהֶם. שֶׁנֶּאֱמַר וְאוֹתָנוּ הוֹצִיא מִשָּׁם. לְמַעַן הָבִיא אֹתָנוּ לָתֶת לָנוּ אֶת הָאָרֶץ אֲשֶׁר נִשְׁבַּע לַאֲבוֹתֵינוּ:

The matzos are covered and the cup is lifted and held until it is to be drunk. According to some customs, however, the cup is put down after the following paragraph, in which case the matzos should once more be uncovered. If this custom is followed, the matzos are to be covered and the cup raised again upon reaching the blessing אֲשֶׁר גְּאָלָנוּ, *Who has redeemed us (p.46).*

offering for HASHEM, Who passed over the houses of the children of Israel in Egypt when He struck the Egyptians and spared our houses; and the people bowed down and prostrated themselves.'

The middle matzah is lifted and displayed while the following paragraph is recited.

Matzah — Why do we eat this unleavened bread? — Because the dough of our fathers did not have time to become leavened before the King of Kings, the Holy One, Blessed is He, revealed Himself to them and redeemed them, as it is written (Exodus 12:39): They baked the dough which they had brought out of Egypt into unleavened bread, for it had not fermented, because they were driven out of Egypt and could not delay, nor had they prepared any provisions for the way.

The matzah alludes to the speed with which He accomplished the Exodus when the proper time arrived.

The maror is lifted and displayed while the following paragraph is recited.

Maror — Why do we eat this bitter herb? — Because the Egyptians embittered the lives of our fathers in Egypt, as it says (Exodus 1:14): They embittered their lives with hard labor, with mortar and bricks, and with all manner of labor in the field: whatever service they made them perform was with hard labor.

And the maror (bitter herbs) symbolize our bitter lot under the Egyptians.

In every generation it is one's duty to regard himself as though he personally had gone out from Egypt, as it is written (Exodus 13:8): You shall tell your son on that day: 'It was because of this that HASHEM did for "me" when I went out of Egypt.' It was not only our fathers whom the Holy One redeemed from slavery; we, too, were redeemed with them, as it is written (Deut. 6:23): He brought "us" out from there so that He might take us to the land which He had promised to our fathers.

The memorials of the night must evoke a feeling of personal relief from suffering. Not only our ancestors, but also we were redeemed. We should feel as though we too were slaves and then redeemed.

The matzos are covered and the cup is lifted and held until it is to be drunk. According to some customs, however, the cup is put down after the following paragraph, in which case the matzos should once more be uncovered. If this custom is followed, the matzos are to be covered and the cup raised again upon reaching the blessing אֲשֶׁר גְּאָלָנוּ, *Who has redeemed us (p.46).*

45 □ THE FAMILY HAGGADAH

לְפִיכָךְ אֲנַחְנוּ חַיָּבִים לְהוֹדוֹת לְהַלֵּל לְשַׁבֵּחַ לְפָאֵר לְרוֹמֵם לְהַדֵּר לְבָרֵךְ לְעַלֵּה וּלְקַלֵּס לְמִי שֶׁעָשָׂה לַאֲבוֹתֵינוּ וְלָנוּ אֶת כָּל הַנִּסִּים הָאֵלוּ הוֹצִיאָנוּ מֵעַבְדוּת לְחֵרוּת מִיָּגוֹן לְשִׂמְחָה וּמֵאֵבֶל לְיוֹם טוֹב וּמֵאֲפֵלָה לְאוֹר גָּדוֹל וּמִשִּׁעְבּוּד לִגְאֻלָּה וְנֹאמַר לְפָנָיו שִׁירָה חֲדָשָׁה הַלְלוּיָהּ:

הַלְלוּיָהּ הַלְלוּ עַבְדֵי יהוה הַלְלוּ אֶת שֵׁם יהוה: יְהִי שֵׁם יהוה מְבֹרָךְ. מֵעַתָּה וְעַד עוֹלָם: מִמִּזְרַח שֶׁמֶשׁ עַד מְבוֹאוֹ מְהֻלָּל שֵׁם יהוה: רָם עַל כָּל גּוֹיִם יהוה. עַל הַשָּׁמַיִם כְּבוֹדוֹ: מִי כַּיהוה אֱלֹהֵינוּ. הַמַּגְבִּיהִי לָשָׁבֶת: הַמַּשְׁפִּילִי לִרְאוֹת בַּשָּׁמַיִם וּבָאָרֶץ: מְקִימִי מֵעָפָר דָּל. מֵאַשְׁפֹּת יָרִים אֶבְיוֹן: לְהוֹשִׁיבִי עִם נְדִיבִים. עִם נְדִיבֵי עַמּוֹ: מוֹשִׁיבִי עֲקֶרֶת הַבַּיִת אֵם הַבָּנִים שְׂמֵחָה הַלְלוּיָהּ:

בְּצֵאת יִשְׂרָאֵל מִמִּצְרָיִם בֵּית יַעֲקֹב מֵעַם לֹעֵז: הָיְתָה יְהוּדָה לְקָדְשׁוֹ יִשְׂרָאֵל מַמְשְׁלוֹתָיו: הַיָּם רָאָה וַיָּנֹס. הַיַּרְדֵּן יִסֹּב לְאָחוֹר: הֶהָרִים רָקְדוּ כְאֵילִים. גְּבָעוֹת כִּבְנֵי צֹאן: מַה לְּךָ הַיָּם כִּי תָנוּס. הַיַּרְדֵּן תִּסֹּב לְאָחוֹר: הֶהָרִים תִּרְקְדוּ כְאֵילִים. גְּבָעוֹת כִּבְנֵי צֹאן: מִלִּפְנֵי אָדוֹן חוּלִי אָרֶץ. מִלִּפְנֵי אֱלוֹהַּ יַעֲקֹב: הַהֹפְכִי הַצּוּר אֲגַם מָיִם. חַלָּמִישׁ לְמַעְיְנוֹ מָיִם:

According to all customs the cup is lifted and the matzohs covered during the recitation of this blessing. (On Saturday night the phrase in parentheses substitutes for the preceding phrase).

בָּרוּךְ אַתָּה יהוה אֱלֹהֵינוּ מֶלֶךְ הָעוֹלָם אֲשֶׁר גְּאָלָנוּ וְגָאַל אֶת אֲבוֹתֵינוּ מִמִּצְרָיִם וְהִגִּיעָנוּ הַלַּיְלָה הַזֶּה לֶאֱכָל בּוֹ מַצָּה וּמָרוֹר. כֵּן יהוה אֱלֹהֵינוּ וֵאלֹהֵי אֲבוֹתֵינוּ יַגִּיעֵנוּ

Therefore, we must offer thanks. For the many manifestations of our redemption we shall now sing God's praises.

Therefore it is our duty to thank, praise, pay tribute, glorify, exalt, honor, bless, extol, and acclaim Him Who performed all these miracles for our fathers and for us. He brought us forth from slavery to freedom, from grief to joy, from mourning to festivity, from darkness to great light, and from servitude to redemption. Let us, therefore, recite a new song before Him! Halleluyah!

We are no longer Pharaoh's slaves; our obligations are soley to the One who elevated us from our lowly stature in Egypt and endowed us with nobility.

Halleluyah! Praise, you servants of HASHEM, praise the Name of HASHEM. Blessed be the Name of HASHEM from now and forever. From the rising of the sun to its setting, HASHEM's Name is praised. High above all nations is HASHEM, above the heavens is His glory. Who is like HASHEM, our God, Who is enthroned on high, yet deigns to look upon heaven and earth? He raises the destitute from the dust, from the trash heaps He lifts the needy — to seat them with nobles, with the nobles of His people. He transforms the barren wife into a glad mother of children. Halleluyah! (Psalms 113).

The laws of nature were subverted during the Exodus. Sea and mountain fled to allow God and His nation to pass.

When Israel went forth from Egypt, Jacob's household from a people of alien tongue, Judah became His sanctuary, Israel His dominion. The Sea saw and fled; the Jordan turned backward. The mountains skipped like rams, and the hills like young lambs. What ails you, O Sea, that you flee? O Jordan, that you turn backward? O mountains, that you skip like rams? O hills, like young lambs? Before HASHEM's presence — tremble, O earth, before the presence of the God of Jacob, Who turns the rock into a pond of water, the flint into a flowing fountain (Psalms 114).

According to all customs the cup is lifted and the matzohs covered during the recitation of this blessing. (On Saturday night the phrase in parentheses substitutes for the preceding phrase).

Blessed are You, HASHEM our God, King of the universe, Who redeemed us and redeemed our ancestors from Egypt and enabled us to reach this night that we may eat matzah and maror. So, HASHEM our God and God of our fathers, bring us also to future

47 □ THE FAMILY HAGGADAH

לְמוֹעֲדִים וְלִרְגָלִים אֲחֵרִים הַבָּאִים לִקְרָאתֵנוּ
לְשָׁלוֹם שְׂמֵחִים בְּבִנְיַן עִירֶךָ וְשָׂשִׂים בַּעֲבוֹדָתֶךָ
וְנֹאכַל שָׁם מִן הַזְּבָחִים וּמִן הַפְּסָחִים (מִן
הַפְּסָחִים וּמִן הַזְּבָחִים) אֲשֶׁר יַגִּיעַ דָּמָם עַל קִיר
מִזְבַּחֲךָ לְרָצוֹן וְנוֹדֶה לְךָ שִׁיר חָדָשׁ עַל גְּאֻלָּתֵנוּ
וְעַל פְּדוּת נַפְשֵׁנוּ. בָּרוּךְ אַתָּה יהוה גָּאַל
יִשְׂרָאֵל:

בָּרוּךְ אַתָּה יהוה אֱלֹהֵינוּ מֶלֶךְ הָעוֹלָם
בּוֹרֵא פְּרִי הַגָּפֶן:

The second cup is drunk while leaning on the left side — preferably the entire cup, but at least most of it.

The hands are washed for matzah and the following blessing is recited. It is preferable to bring water and a basin to the head of the household at the Seder table.

בָּרוּךְ אַתָּה יהוה אֱלֹהֵינוּ מֶלֶךְ הָעוֹלָם
אֲשֶׁר קִדְּשָׁנוּ בְּמִצְוֹתָיו וְצִוָּנוּ עַל
נְטִילַת יָדָיִם:

מוֹצִיא

The following two blessings are recited over matzah; the first is recited over matzah as food, and the second for the special mitzvah of eating matzah on the night of Passover. [The latter blessing is to be made with the intention that it also apply to the 'sandwich' and the afikoman.]

The head of the household raises all the matzos on the seder plate and recites the following blessing:

בָּרוּךְ אַתָּה יהוה אֱלֹהֵינוּ מֶלֶךְ הָעוֹלָם
הַמּוֹצִיא לֶחֶם מִן הָאָרֶץ:

The bottom matzah is put down and the following blessing is recited while the top (whole) matzah and the middle (broken) piece are still raised.

The Exodus was not an end unto itself, but a prelude to our entry into the Holy Land and the erection of the Temple in Jerusalem. Thus, the formal thanksgiving blessing for the redemption includes a prayer for a rebuilt Temple and the resumption of our worship there.

festivals and holidays in peace, gladdened in the rebuilding of Your city, and joyful at Your service. There we shall eat of the offerings and Passover sacrifices (of the Passover sacrifices and offerings) whose blood will gain the sides of Your altar for gracious acceptance. We shall then sing a new song of praise to You for our redemption and for the liberation of our souls. Blessed are You, HASHEM, Who has redeemed Israel.

Blessed are You, HASHEM our God, King of the universe, Who creates the fruit of the vine.

The second cup is drunk while leaning on the left side — preferably the entire cup, but at least most of it.

RACHTZAH

The hands are washed for matzah and the following blessing is recited. It is preferable to bring water and a basin to the head of the household at the Seder table.

Blessed are You, HASHEM our God, King of the universe, Who has sanctified us with His commandments, and has commanded us concerning the washing of the hands.

MOTZI

The following two blessings are recited over matzah; the first is recited over matzah as food, and the second for the special mitzvah of eating matzah on the night of Passover. [The latter blessing is to be made with the intention that it also apply to the 'sandwich' and the afikoman.]

The head of the household raises all the matzos on the seder plate and recites the following blessing:

The blessing over matzah as food, as the more common benediction, is recited first.

Blessed are You, HASHEM our God, King of the universe, Who brings forth bread from the earth.

The bottom matzah is put down and the following blessing is recited while the top (whole) matzah and the middle (broken) piece are still raised.

49 □ THE FAMILY HAGGADAH

בָּרוּךְ אַתָּה יהוה אֱלֹהֵינוּ מֶלֶךְ הָעוֹלָם אֲשֶׁר קִדְּשָׁנוּ בְּמִצְוֹתָיו וְצִוָּנוּ עַל אֲכִילַת מַצָּה:

Each participant is required to eat an amount of matzah equal in volume to an egg. Since it is impossible to provide a sufficient amount of matzah from the two matzos for all members of the household, other matzos should be available at the table from which to complete the required amounts. However, each participant should receive a piece from each of the top two matzos. The matzos are to be eaten while reclining on the left side and without delay; they need not be dipped in salt.

The head of the household takes a half-egg volume of maror, dips it into charoses, shakes off the charoses, and gives each participant a like amount. The following blessing is recited with the intention that it also apply to the maror of the 'sandwich'. The maror is eaten without reclining, and without delay.

בָּרוּךְ אַתָּה יהוה אֱלֹהֵינוּ מֶלֶךְ הָעוֹלָם אֲשֶׁר קִדְּשָׁנוּ בְּמִצְוֹתָיו וְצִוָּנוּ עַל אֲכִילַת מָרוֹר:

כּוֹרֵךְ

The bottom (thus far unbroken) matzah is now taken. From it, with the addition of other matzos, each participant receives a half-egg volume of matzah along with an equal volume portion of maror (dipped into charoses which is shaken off). The following paragraph is recited and the 'sandwich' is eaten while reclining.

זֵכֶר לְמִקְדָּשׁ כְּהִלֵּל. כֵּן עָשָׂה הִלֵּל בִּזְמַן שֶׁבֵּית הַמִּקְדָּשׁ הָיָה קַיָּם. הָיָה כּוֹרֵךְ (פֶּסַח) מַצָּה וּמָרוֹר וְאוֹכֵל בְּיַחַד. לְקַיֵּם מַה שֶׁנֶּאֱמַר עַל מַצּוֹת וּמְרֹרִים יֹאכְלֻהוּ:

MATZAH

But the matzah of Pesach is no mere substitute for bread. Its use is in fulfillment of a commandment, and requires a blessing of its own.

B lessed are You, HASHEM our God, King of the universe, Who has sanctified us with His commandments, and has commanded us concerning the eating of the matzah.

Each participant is required to eat an amount of matzah equal in volume to an egg. Since it is impossible to provide a sufficient amount of matzah from the two matzos for all members of the household, other matzos should be available at the table from which to complete the required amounts. However, each participant should receive a piece from each of the top two matzos. The matzos are to be eaten while reclining on the left side and without delay; they need not be dipped in salt.

MAROR

The maror symbolizes the bitterness inflicted by the Egyptians. Charoses (literally, potter's clay) resembles the mortar with which our ancestors built Egyptian cities.

Additionally, the apples, nuts, cinnamon and other ingredients of the charoses are used in Song of Songs as symbols of the qualities of the Jewish people.

The head of the household takes a half-egg volume of maror, dips it into charoses, shakes off the charoses, and gives each participant a like amount. The following blessing is recited with the intention that it also apply to the maror of the 'sandwich'. The maror is eaten without reclining, and without delay.

B lessed are You, HASHEM our God, King of the universe, Who has sanctified us with His commandments, and has commanded us concerning the eating of Maror.

KORECH

The bottom (thus far unbroken) matzah is now taken. From it, with the addition of other matzos, each participant receives a half-egg volume of matzah along with an equal volume portion of maror (dipped into charoses which is shaken off). The following paragraph is recited and the 'sandwich' is eaten while reclining.

I n rememberance of the Temple we do as Hillel did in Temple times: he would combine Passover offering, matzah and maror in a sandwich and eat them together, to fulfill what is written in the Torah (Numbers 9:11): They shall eat it with matzos and bitter herbs.

51 □ THE FAMILY HAGGADAH

שֻׁלְחָן עוֹרֵךְ

The meal should be eaten in a combination of joy and solemnity, for the meal, too, is part of the Seder service. While it is desirable that zemiros and discussion of the laws and events of Passover be part of the meal, extraneous conversation should be avoided. It should be remembered that the afikoman must be eaten while there is still some appetite for it. In fact, if one is so sated that he must literally force himself to eat it, he is not credited with the performance of the mitzvah of afikoman. Therefore, it is unwise to eat more than a moderate amount during the meal.

צָפוּן

From the afikoman matzah (and from additional matzos to make up the required amount) a half-egg volume portion — according to some, a full egg's volume portion — is given to each participant. It should be eaten before midnight, while reclining, without delay, and uninterruptedly. Nothing may be eaten or drunk after the afikoman (with the exception of water and the like) except for the last two Seder cups of wine.

בָּרֵךְ

The third cup is poured and Bircas HaMazon (Grace After Meals) is recited. According to some customs, the Cup of Elijah, is poured at this point.

שִׁיר הַמַּעֲלוֹת בְּשׁוּב יהוה אֶת שִׁיבַת צִיּוֹן הָיִינוּ כְּחֹלְמִים: אָז יִמָּלֵא שְׂחוֹק פִּינוּ וּלְשׁוֹנֵנוּ רִנָּה אָז יֹאמְרוּ בַגּוֹיִם הִגְדִּיל יהוה לַעֲשׂוֹת עִם אֵלֶּה: הִגְדִּיל יהוה לַעֲשׂוֹת עִמָּנוּ הָיִינוּ שְׂמֵחִים: שׁוּבָה יהוה אֶת שְׁבִיתֵנוּ כַּאֲפִיקִים בַּנֶּגֶב: הַזֹּרְעִים בְּדִמְעָה בְּרִנָּה יִקְצֹרוּ: הָלוֹךְ יֵלֵךְ וּבָכֹה נֹשֵׂא מֶשֶׁךְ הַזָּרַע בֹּא יָבֹא בְרִנָּה נֹשֵׂא אֲלֻמֹּתָיו:

SHULCHAN ORECH

The meal should be eaten in a combination of joy and solemnity, for the meal, too, is part of the Seder service. While it is desirable that zemiros and discussion of the laws and events of Passover be part of the meal, extraneous conversation should be avoided. It should be remembered that the afikoman must be eaten while there is still some appetite for it. In fact, if one is so sated that he must literally force himself to eat it, he is not credited with the performance of the mitzvah of afikoman. Therefore, it is unwise to eat more than a moderate amount during the meal.

TZAFUN

We allow the taste of the afikoman ("desert") to linger in our mouths; for the afikoman — a piece of bland matzah — signifies that it is not the sweetness of the food which whets our palate, but the observance of mitzvos which is "sweeter than honey dripping from the combs."

From the afikoman matzah (and from additional matzos to make up the required amount) a half-egg volume portion — according to some, a full egg's volume portion — is given to each participant. It should be eaten before midnight, while reclining, without delay, and uninterruptedly. Nothing may be eaten or drunk after the afikoman (with the exception of water and the like) except for the last two Seder cups of wine.

BARECH

The third cup is poured and Bircas HaMazon (Grace After Meals) is recited. According to some customs, the Cup of Elijah, is poured at this point.

On all festive days the Grace is prefaced with Psalm 126 which describes the joys of redemption.

A Song of Ascents. When HASHEM brings back the exiles to Zion, we will have been like dreamers. Then our mouth will be filled with laughter, and our tongue with glad song. Then will it be said among the nations: HASHEM has done great things for them. HASHEM has done great things for us, and we rejoiced. Restore our captives, HASHEM, like streams in the dryland. Those who sow in tears shall reap in joy. Though the farmer bears the measure of seed to the field in tears, he shall come home with joy, bearing his sheaves (Psalm 126).

53 □ THE FAMILY HAGGADAH

*If three or more males, aged thirteen or older, participated in the meal, the
leader is required to formally invite the others to join him in the recitation of
Grace after Meals. Following is the 'Zimun,' or formal invitation.*

The leader begins:

רַבּוֹתַי נְבָרֵךְ.

The group responds:

יְהִי שֵׁם יהוה מְבֹרָךְ מֵעַתָּה וְעַד עוֹלָם.

The leader continues:

יְהִי שֵׁם יהוה מְבֹרָךְ מֵעַתָּה וְעַד עוֹלָם.

If ten men join in the Zimun, אֱלֹהֵינוּ, *our God (in parentheses) is included.*

בִּרְשׁוּת מָרָנָן וְרַבָּנָן וְרַבּוֹתַי נְבָרֵךְ (אֱלֹהֵינוּ) שֶׁאָכַלְנוּ מִשֶּׁלּוֹ.

The group responds:

בָּרוּךְ (אֱלֹהֵינוּ) שֶׁאָכַלְנוּ מִשֶּׁלּוֹ וּבְטוּבוֹ חָיִינוּ.

The leader concludes:

בָּרוּךְ (אֱלֹהֵינוּ) שֶׁאָכַלְנוּ מִשֶּׁלּוֹ וּבְטוּבוֹ חָיִינוּ.

The following line is recited if ten men join in the Zimun.

בָּרוּךְ הוּא וּבָרוּךְ שְׁמוֹ:

בָּרוּךְ אַתָּה יהוה אֱלֹהֵינוּ מֶלֶךְ הָעוֹלָם הַזָּן
אֶת הָעוֹלָם כֻּלּוֹ בְּטוּבוֹ בְּחֵן בְּחֶסֶד
וּבְרַחֲמִים הוּא נֹתֵן לֶחֶם לְכָל בָּשָׂר כִּי לְעוֹלָם
חַסְדּוֹ. וּבְטוּבוֹ הַגָּדוֹל תָּמִיד לֹא חָסַר לָנוּ וְאַל
יֶחְסַר לָנוּ מָזוֹן לְעוֹלָם וָעֶד. בַּעֲבוּר שְׁמוֹ הַגָּדוֹל
כִּי הוּא אֵל זָן וּמְפַרְנֵס לַכֹּל וּמֵטִיב לַכֹּל וּמֵכִין
מָזוֹן לְכָל בְּרִיּוֹתָיו אֲשֶׁר בָּרָא. בָּרוּךְ אַתָּה יהוה
הַזָּן אֶת הַכֹּל:

נוֹדֶה לְךָ יהוה אֱלֹהֵינוּ עַל שֶׁהִנְחַלְתָּ
לַאֲבוֹתֵינוּ אֶרֶץ חֶמְדָּה טוֹבָה וּרְחָבָה.
וְעַל שֶׁהוֹצֵאתָנוּ יהוה אֱלֹהֵינוּ מֵאֶרֶץ מִצְרַיִם
וּפְדִיתָנוּ מִבֵּית עֲבָדִים וְעַל בְּרִיתְךָ שֶׁחָתַמְתָּ
בִּבְשָׂרֵנוּ וְעַל תּוֹרָתְךָ שֶׁלִּמַּדְתָּנוּ וְעַל חֻקֶּיךָ
שֶׁהוֹדַעְתָּנוּ וְעַל חַיִּים חֵן וָחֶסֶד שֶׁחוֹנַנְתָּנוּ וְעַל
אֲכִילַת מָזוֹן שָׁאַתָּה זָן וּמְפַרְנֵס אוֹתָנוּ תָּמִיד
בְּכָל יוֹם וּבְכָל עֵת וּבְכָל שָׁעָה:

הגדה של פסח □ 54

If three or more males, aged thirteen or older, participated in the meal, the leader is required to formally invite the others to join him in the recitation of Grace after Meals. Following is the 'Zimun,' or formal invitation.

The leader begins:

Gentlemen let us bless.

The Psalmist called to his people, "Declare the greatness of HASHEM with me, and let us exalt His Name together!" Accordingly the Sages ordained that when three eat together, one of them should declare God's greatness, and the others respond together in praise of His Name.

The group responds:

Blessed is the Name of HASHEM from this moment and forever!

The leader continues:

Blessed is the Name of HASHEM from this moment and forever!

If ten men join in the Zimun, אֱלֹהֵינוּ, *our God (in parentheses) is included.*

With the permission of the distinguished people present let us bless [our God] for we have eaten from what is His.

The group responds:

Blessed is He [our God] of Whose we have eaten and through Whose goodness we live.

The leader continues:

Blessed is He [our God] of Whose we have eaten and through Whose goodness we live.

The following line is recited if ten men join in the Zimun.

Blessed is He and blessed is His Name.

Blessed are You, HASHEM, our God, King of the universe, Who nourishes the entire world; in His goodness, with grace, with lovingkindness, and with mercy. He gives nourishment to all flesh, for His lovingkindness is eternal. And through His great goodness nourishment was never lacking to us and may it never be lacking to us forever. For the sake of His Great Name, because He is the God Who nourishes and sustains all, and benefits all, and He prepares food for all of His creatures which He has created. Blessed are You, HASHEM, Who nourishes all.

Moses composed this blessing in gratitude for the manna with which God sustained the Israelites in the Wilderness. It was adopted as the first of the four which make up Bircas HaMazon recited after all meals.

We thank You, HASHEM, our God, because You have given to our forefathers as a heritage a desirable, good and spacious land; because You removed us, HASHEM, our God, from the land of Egypt and You redeemed us from the house of bondage; for Your covenant which You sealed in our flesh; for Your Torah which You taught us and for Your statutes which You made known to us; for life, grace, and lovingkindness which You granted us; and for the provision of food with which You nourish and sustain us constantly, in every day, in every season, and in every hour.

"We Thank You" was written by Joshua when he led the nation across the Jordan into the "desirable, good and spacious land," "flowing with milk and honey."

55 ☐ THE FAMILY HAGGADAH

וְעַל הַכֹּל יהוה אֱלֹהֵינוּ אֲנַחְנוּ מוֹדִים
לָךְ וּמְבָרְכִים אוֹתָךְ יִתְבָּרַךְ
שִׁמְךָ בְּפִי כָּל חַי תָּמִיד לְעוֹלָם וָעֶד. כַּכָּתוּב
וְאָכַלְתָּ וְשָׂבָעְתָּ וּבֵרַכְתָּ אֶת יהוה אֱלֹהֶיךָ עַל
הָאָרֶץ הַטֹּבָה אֲשֶׁר נָתַן לָךְ. בָּרוּךְ אַתָּה יהוה
עַל הָאָרֶץ וְעַל הַמָּזוֹן:

רַחֵם (נָא) יהוה אֱלֹהֵינוּ עַל יִשְׂרָאֵל עַמֶּךָ
וְעַל יְרוּשָׁלַיִם עִירֶךָ וְעַל צִיּוֹן מִשְׁכַּן
כְּבוֹדֶךָ וְעַל מַלְכוּת בֵּית דָּוִד מְשִׁיחֶךָ וְעַל הַבַּיִת
הַגָּדוֹל וְהַקָּדוֹשׁ שֶׁנִּקְרָא שִׁמְךָ עָלָיו. אֱלֹהֵינוּ
אָבִינוּ רְעֵנוּ זוּנֵנוּ פַּרְנְסֵנוּ וְכַלְכְּלֵנוּ וְהַרְוִיחֵנוּ
וְהַרְוַח לָנוּ יהוה אֱלֹהֵינוּ מְהֵרָה מִכָּל צָרוֹתֵינוּ.
וְנָא אַל תַּצְרִיכֵנוּ יהוה אֱלֹהֵינוּ לֹא לִידֵי מַתְּנַת
בָּשָׂר וָדָם וְלֹא לִידֵי הַלְוָאָתָם כִּי אִם לְיָדְךָ
הַמְּלֵאָה הַפְּתוּחָה הַקְּדוֹשָׁה וְהָרְחָבָה שֶׁלֹּא
נֵבוֹשׁ וְלֹא נִכָּלֵם לְעוֹלָם וָעֶד:

On the Sabbath add the following paragraph.

רְצֵה וְהַחֲלִיצֵנוּ יהוה אֱלֹהֵינוּ בְּמִצְוֹתֶיךָ וּבְמִצְוַת יוֹם
הַשְּׁבִיעִי הַשַּׁבָּת הַגָּדוֹל וְהַקָּדוֹשׁ הַזֶּה כִּי יוֹם
זֶה גָּדוֹל וְקָדוֹשׁ הוּא לְפָנֶיךָ לִשְׁבָּת בּוֹ וְלָנוּחַ בּוֹ
בְּאַהֲבָה כְּמִצְוַת רְצוֹנֶךָ וּבִרְצוֹנְךָ הָנִיחַ לָנוּ יהוה
אֱלֹהֵינוּ שֶׁלֹּא תְהֵא צָרָה וְיָגוֹן וַאֲנָחָה בְּיוֹם מְנוּחָתֵנוּ
וְהַרְאֵנוּ יהוה אֱלֹהֵינוּ בְּנֶחָמַת צִיּוֹן עִירֶךָ וּבְבִנְיַן
יְרוּשָׁלַיִם עִיר קָדְשֶׁךָ כִּי אַתָּה הוּא בַּעַל הַיְשׁוּעוֹת
וּבַעַל הַנֶּחָמוֹת:

אֱלֹהֵינוּ וֵאלֹהֵי אֲבוֹתֵינוּ יַעֲלֶה וְיָבֹא וְיַגִּיעַ
וְיֵרָאֶה וְיֵרָצֶה וְיִשָּׁמַע וְיִפָּקֵד
וְיִזָּכֵר זִכְרוֹנֵנוּ וּפִקְדוֹנֵנוּ וְזִכְרוֹן אֲבוֹתֵינוּ וְזִכְרוֹן
מָשִׁיחַ בֶּן דָּוִד עַבְדֶּךָ וְזִכְרוֹן יְרוּשָׁלַיִם עִיר

הגדה של פסח ☐ 56

For all, HASHEM, our God, we thank You and bless You. May Your Name be blessed continuously forever by the mouth of all the living. As it is written (Deuteronomy 8:10): 'And you shall eat and be satisfied and bless HASHEM, your God, for the good land which He gave you.' Blessed are You, HASHEM, for the land and for the food.

"Have Mercy" was composed by King David who referred to "Your people Israel ... Your city Jerusalem ..." Upon completing construction of the Temple, King Solomon added "the great and holy House upon which Your Name is called."

Have mercy (we beg You) HASHEM, our God, on Your people Israel, on Your city Jerusalem, on Zion the resting place of Your Glory, on the monarchy of the house of David, Your anointed, and on the great and holy House upon which Your Name is called. Our God, our Father — tend us, nourish us, sustain us, support us, relieve us; HASHEM, our God, grant us speedy relief from all our troubles. Please, HASHEM, our God, make us not needful of the gifts of human hands nor of their loans — but only of Your Hand that is full, open, holy, and generous, that we not feel inner shame or be humiliated for ever and ever.

On the Sabbath add the following paragraph.

May it please You, HASHEM, our God — give us rest through Your commandments and through the commandment of the seventh day, this great and holy Sabbath. For this day is great and holy before You to rest on it and be content on it in love, as ordained by Your will. May it be Your will, HASHEM, our God, that there be no distress, grief, or lament on this day of our contentment. And show us, HASHEM, our God, the consolation of Zion, Your city, and the rebuilding of Jerusalem, city of Your holiness, for You are the Master of salvations and Master of consolations.

May our lot rise above the ordinary; come before God, reach Him and be noted by Him in the best of lights, worthy of His favor. May He hear the impact on our lives, consider our needs and remember our relationship to Him.

Our God and God of our fathers, may there rise, come, reach, be noted, be favored, be heard, be considered, and be remembered before You — the remembrance and consideration of ourselves, the remembrance of our fathers; the remembrance of Messiah, son of David, Your servant; the remembrance of Jerusalem, Your holy city; and the remembrance of

57 □ THE FAMILY HAGGADAH

קָדְשֶׁךָ וְזִכְרוֹן כָּל עַמְּךָ בֵּית יִשְׂרָאֵל לְפָנֶיךָ
לִפְלֵיטָה לְטוֹבָה לְחֵן וּלְחֶסֶד וּלְרַחֲמִים לְחַיִּים
וּלְשָׁלוֹם בְּיוֹם חַג הַמַּצּוֹת הַזֶּה. זָכְרֵנוּ יהוה
אֱלֹהֵינוּ בּוֹ לְטוֹבָה. וּפָקְדֵנוּ בּוֹ לִבְרָכָה.
וְהוֹשִׁיעֵנוּ בּוֹ לְחַיִּים (טוֹבִים). וּבִדְבַר יְשׁוּעָה
וְרַחֲמִים חוּס וְחָנֵּנוּ וְרַחֵם עָלֵינוּ וְהוֹשִׁיעֵנוּ כִּי
אֵלֶיךָ עֵינֵינוּ כִּי אֵל חַנּוּן וְרַחוּם אָתָּה:

וּבְנֵה יְרוּשָׁלַיִם עִיר הַקֹּדֶשׁ בִּמְהֵרָה בְיָמֵינוּ.
בָּרוּךְ אַתָּה יהוה בּוֹנֵה (בְּרַחֲמָיו)
יְרוּשָׁלָיִם. אָמֵן:

בָּרוּךְ אַתָּה יהוה אֱלֹהֵינוּ מֶלֶךְ הָעוֹלָם
הָאֵל אָבִינוּ מַלְכֵּנוּ אַדִּירֵנוּ בּוֹרְאֵנוּ
גּוֹאֲלֵנוּ יוֹצְרֵנוּ קְדוֹשֵׁנוּ קְדוֹשׁ יַעֲקֹב רוֹעֵנוּ רוֹעֵה
יִשְׂרָאֵל הַמֶּלֶךְ הַטּוֹב וְהַמֵּטִיב לַכֹּל שֶׁבְּכָל יוֹם
וָיוֹם הוּא הֵטִיב הוּא מֵטִיב הוּא יֵיטִיב לָנוּ. הוּא
גְמָלָנוּ הוּא גוֹמְלֵנוּ הוּא יִגְמְלֵנוּ לָעַד לְחֵן
וּלְחֶסֶד וּלְרַחֲמִים וּלְרֶוַח הַצָּלָה וְהַצְלָחָה בְּרָכָה
וִישׁוּעָה נֶחָמָה פַּרְנָסָה וְכַלְכָּלָה וְרַחֲמִים וְחַיִּים
וְשָׁלוֹם וְכָל טוֹב וּמִכָּל טוּב לְעוֹלָם אַל יְחַסְּרֵנוּ:

הָרַחֲמָן הוּא יִמְלוֹךְ עָלֵינוּ לְעוֹלָם וָעֶד.
הָרַחֲמָן הוּא יִתְבָּרַךְ בַּשָּׁמַיִם
וּבָאָרֶץ. הָרַחֲמָן הוּא יִשְׁתַּבַּח לְדוֹר דּוֹרִים
וְיִתְפָּאַר בָּנוּ לָעַד וּלְנֵצַח נְצָחִים וְיִתְהַדַּר בָּנוּ
לָעַד וּלְעוֹלְמֵי עוֹלָמִים. הָרַחֲמָן הוּא יְפַרְנְסֵנוּ
בְּכָבוֹד. הָרַחֲמָן הוּא יִשְׁבּוֹר עֻלֵּנוּ מֵעַל צַוָּארֵנוּ
וְהוּא יוֹלִיכֵנוּ קוֹמְמִיּוּת לְאַרְצֵנוּ. הָרַחֲמָן הוּא
יִשְׁלַח לָנוּ בְּרָכָה מְרֻבָּה בַּבַּיִת הַזֶּה וְעַל שֻׁלְחָן
זֶה שֶׁאָכַלְנוּ עָלָיו. הָרַחֲמָן הוּא יִשְׁלַח לָנוּ אֶת

Your entire people, the House of Israel — for deliverance, for well-being, for grace, for lovingkindness, and for mercy, for life and for peace on this day of the Festival of Matzos. Remember us on it, HASHEM, our God, for goodness, consider us on it for blessing, and help us on it for (good) life. Concerning salvation and mercy, have pity, show grace and be merciful upon us and help us. For our eyes are turned to You; for You are the Almighty, gracious, and generous.

R ebuild Jerusalem, the Holy City, soon in our days. Blessed are You, HASHEM, Who rebuilds Jerusalem (in His mercy). Amen.

It is insufficient to thank God for His graciousness and beneficence to past generations. We must be aware that His goodness and bounty are daily, constant occurrences — and will always be so.

B lessed are You, HASHEM our God, King of the universe, the Almighty, our Father, our King, our Sovereign, our Creator, our Redeemer, our Maker, our Holy One, Holy One of Jacob, our Shepherd, the Shepherd of Israel, the good and beneficent King. For every single day He did good, does good, and will do good to us. He was bountiful with us, is bountiful with us, and will forever be bountiful with us — with grace and with lovingkindness and with mercy, with relief, salvation, success, blessing, help, consolation, sustenance, support, mercy, life, peace, and all good; and of all good things may He never deprive us.

T he compassionate One! May He reign over us forever. The compassionate One! May He be blessed on heaven and on earth. The compassionate One! May He be praised throughout all generations, may He be glorified through us to the ultimate ends, and be honored through us to the inscrutable everlasting. The compassionate One! May He sustain us in honor. The compassionate One! May He break the yoke of oppression from our necks and guide us erect to our Land. The compassionate One! May He send us abundant blessing to this house and upon this table at which we have eaten. The compassionate One! May He send us Elijah, the Prophet — may he be

59 ☐ THE FAMILY HAGGADAH

אֵלִיָּהוּ הַנָּבִיא זָכוּר לַטּוֹב וִיבַשֶּׂר לָנוּ בְּשׂוֹרוֹת
טוֹבוֹת יְשׁוּעוֹת וְנֶחָמוֹת. הָרַחֲמָן הוּא יְבָרֵךְ

Guests recite the following.
Children at their parents' table add words in parentheses.

אֶת (אָבִי מוֹרִי) בַּעַל הַבַּיִת הַזֶּה
וְאֶת (אִמִּי מוֹרָתִי) בַּעֲלַת הַבַּיִת הַזֶּה.

Those eating at their own table recite the following, adding the appropriate
parenthesized phrases:

אוֹתִי (וְאֶת אִשְׁתִּי/בַּעְלִי. וְאֶת זַרְעִי)
וְאֶת כָּל אֲשֶׁר לִי.

All guests recite the following:

אוֹתָם וְאֶת בֵּיתָם וְאֶת זַרְעָם
וְאֶת כָּל אֲשֶׁר לָהֶם

All continue here:

אוֹתָנוּ וְאֶת כָּל אֲשֶׁר לָנוּ כְּמוֹ שֶׁנִּתְבָּרְכוּ
אֲבוֹתֵינוּ אַבְרָהָם יִצְחָק וְיַעֲקֹב בַּכֹּל מִכֹּל כֹּל כֵּן
יְבָרֵךְ אוֹתָנוּ כֻּלָּנוּ יַחַד בִּבְרָכָה שְׁלֵמָה וְנֹאמַר
אָמֵן:

בַּמָּרוֹם יְלַמְּדוּ עֲלֵיהֶם וְעָלֵינוּ זְכוּת שֶׁתְּהֵא
לְמִשְׁמֶרֶת שָׁלוֹם. וְנִשָּׂא בְרָכָה
מֵאֵת יהוה וּצְדָקָה מֵאֱלֹהֵי יִשְׁעֵנוּ וְנִמְצָא חֵן
וְשֵׂכֶל טוֹב בְּעֵינֵי אֱלֹהִים וְאָדָם:

On the Sabbath add the following sentence:

הָרַחֲמָן הוּא יַנְחִילֵנוּ יוֹם שֶׁכֻּלּוֹ שַׁבָּת וּמְנוּחָה לְחַיֵּי
הָעוֹלָמִים:

The words in parentheses are added on the two Seder nights in some com-
munities.

הָרַחֲמָן הוּא יַנְחִילֵנוּ יוֹם שֶׁכֻּלּוֹ טוֹב. (יוֹם
שֶׁכֻּלּוֹ אָרוּךְ. יוֹם שֶׁצַּדִּיקִים
יוֹשְׁבִים וְעַטְרוֹתֵיהֶם בְּרָאשֵׁיהֶם וְנֶהֱנִים מִזִּיו
הַשְּׁכִינָה וִיהִי חֶלְקֵנוּ עִמָּהֶם):

remembered for good — to proclaim to us good tidings, salvations, and consolations. The compassionate One! May He bless

Guests recite the following.
Children at their parents' table add the words in parentheses

(my father, my teacher) the master of this house, and (my mother, my teacher) lady of this house,

Those eating at their own table recite the following, adding the appropriate parenthesized phrases:

me (my wife/husband and family) and all that is mine,

All guests recite the following:

them, their house, their family, and all that is theirs,

All continue here:

The Patriarchs were blessed in every possible way. "And HASHEM blessed Abraham in everything." Isaac declared, "I have partaken from everything." And Jacob said, "God has been gracious to me and I have everything." So may we be blessed.

ours and all that is ours — just as our forefathers Abraham, Isaac, and Jacob were blessed in everything, from everything, with everything. So may He bless us all together with a perfect blessing. And let us say: Amen!

On high, may merit be pleaded upon them and upon us, for a safeguard of peace. May we receive a blessing from HASHEM and just kindness from the God of our salvation, and find favor and understanding in the eyes of God and man.

On the Sabbath add the following sentence:

The compassionate One! May He cause us to inherit the day which will be completely a Sabbath and rest day for eternal life.

The words in parentheses are added on the two Seder nights in some communities.

The compassionate One! May He cause us to inherit that day which is altogether good, (that everlasting day, the day when the just will sit with crowns on their heads, enjoying the reflection of God's Majesty — and may our portion be with them!).

61 □ THE FAMILY HAGGADAH

הָרַחֲמָן הוּא יְזַכֵּנוּ לִימוֹת הַמָּשִׁיחַ וּלְחַיֵּי הָעוֹלָם הַבָּא. מַגְדִּיל יְשׁוּעוֹת מַלְכּוֹ וְעֹשֶׂה חֶסֶד לִמְשִׁיחוֹ לְדָוִד וּלְזַרְעוֹ עַד עוֹלָם. עֹשֶׂה שָׁלוֹם בִּמְרוֹמָיו הוּא יַעֲשֶׂה שָׁלוֹם עָלֵינוּ וְעַל כָּל יִשְׂרָאֵל. וְאִמְרוּ אָמֵן:

יְראוּ אֶת יהוה קְדֹשָׁיו כִּי אֵין מַחְסוֹר לִירֵאָיו. כְּפִירִים רָשׁוּ וְרָעֵבוּ וְדֹרְשֵׁי יהוה לֹא יַחְסְרוּ כָל טוֹב. הוֹדוּ לַיהוה כִּי טוֹב כִּי לְעוֹלָם חַסְדּוֹ. פּוֹתֵחַ אֶת יָדֶךָ וּמַשְׂבִּיעַ לְכָל חַי רָצוֹן. בָּרוּךְ הַגֶּבֶר אֲשֶׁר יִבְטַח בַּיהוה וְהָיָה יהוה מִבְטַחוֹ. נַעַר הָיִיתִי גַּם זָקַנְתִּי וְלֹא רָאִיתִי צַדִּיק נֶעֱזָב וְזַרְעוֹ מְבַקֶּשׁ לָחֶם. יהוה עֹז לְעַמּוֹ יִתֵּן יהוה יְבָרֵךְ אֶת עַמּוֹ בַשָּׁלוֹם:

Upon completion of Bircas Hamazon the blessing over wine is recited and the third cup is drunk while reclining on the left side. It is preferable to drink the entire cup, but at the very least, most of the cup should be drained.

בָּרוּךְ אַתָּה יהוה אֱלֹהֵינוּ מֶלֶךְ הָעוֹלָם בּוֹרֵא פְּרִי הַגָּפֶן:

The fourth cup is poured. According to most customs, the Cup of Elijah is poured at this point, after which the door is opened in accordance with the verse 'It is a guarded night,' and the following paragraph is recited.

שְׁפֹךְ חֲמָתְךָ אֶל הַגּוֹיִם אֲשֶׁר לֹא יְדָעוּךָ וְעַל מַמְלָכוֹת אֲשֶׁר בְּשִׁמְךָ לֹא קָרָאוּ: כִּי אָכַל אֶת יַעֲקֹב וְאֶת נָוֵהוּ הֵשַׁמּוּ: שְׁפָךְ עֲלֵיהֶם זַעֲמֶךָ וַחֲרוֹן אַפְּךָ יַשִּׂיגֵם: תִּרְדֹּף בְּאַף וְתַשְׁמִידֵם מִתַּחַת שְׁמֵי יהוה:

The door is closed and the recitation of the Haggadah is continued.

KADDESH
URECHATZ
KARPAS
YACHATZ
MAGGID
RACHTZAH
MOTZI
MATZAH
MAROR
KORECH
SHULCHAN ORECH
TZAFUN
BARECH
HALLEL
NIRTZAH

The compassionate One! May He make us worthy to attain the days of Messiah and the life of the World to Come. He Who is a tower of salvations to His king and shows loving-kindness to His anointed, to David and his descendants forever. He Who makes harmony in His heavenly heights, may He make harmony for us and for all Israel. Say: Amen!

Fear HASHEM, His holy ones, for those who fear Him feel no deprivation. Young lions may feel want and hunger, but those who seek HASHEM will not lack any good. Give thanks to God for He is good; His lovingkindness is eternal. You open Your hand and satisfy the desire of every living thing. Blessed is the man who trusts in HASHEM, and HASHEM will be his trust. I was a youth and also have aged, and I have not seen a righteous man forsaken, with his children begging for bread. HASHEM will give might to His nation; HASHEM will bless His nation with peace.

Upon completion of Bircas Hamazon the blessing over wine is recited and the third cup is drunk while reclining on the left side. It is preferable to drink the entire cup, but at the very least, most of the cup should be drained.

Blessed are You, HASHEM our God, King of the universe, Who creates the fruit of the vine.

The fourth cup is poured. According to most customs, the Cup of Elijah is poured at this point, after which the door is opened in accordance with the verse 'It is a guarded night,' and the following paragraph is recited.

Past redemption from Egypt was the theme of the part of the Haggadah recited before the meal. Now, the tense switches and the future Messianic redemption is brought to the fore. We open the door, indicating our readiness to receive the Prophet Elijah, herald of the Messiah, as we beseech God to pour His wrath upon those who would play Pharaoh's spiritual successors in oppressing the Jews.

Pour Your wrath upon the nations that do not recognize You and upon the kingdoms that do not invoke Your Name. For they have devoured Jacob and destroyed His Habitation. Pour Your anger upon them and let Your fiery wrath overtake them. Pursue them with wrath and annihilate them from beneath the heavens of HASHEM.

HALLEL

The door is closed and the recitation of the Haggadah is continued.

לֹא לָנוּ יְהוָה לֹא לָנוּ כִּי לְשִׁמְךָ תֵּן כָּבוֹד עַל חַסְדְּךָ עַל אֲמִתֶּךָ: לָמָּה יֹאמְרוּ הַגּוֹיִם אַיֵּה נָא אֱלֹהֵיהֶם: וֵאלֹהֵינוּ בַשָּׁמָיִם כֹּל אֲשֶׁר חָפֵץ עָשָׂה: עֲצַבֵּיהֶם כֶּסֶף וְזָהָב מַעֲשֵׂה יְדֵי אָדָם: פֶּה לָהֶם וְלֹא יְדַבֵּרוּ עֵינַיִם לָהֶם וְלֹא יִרְאוּ: אָזְנַיִם לָהֶם וְלֹא יִשְׁמָעוּ אַף לָהֶם וְלֹא יְרִיחוּן: יְדֵיהֶם וְלֹא יְמִישׁוּן רַגְלֵיהֶם וְלֹא יְהַלֵּכוּ לֹא יֶהְגּוּ בִּגְרוֹנָם: כְּמוֹהֶם יִהְיוּ עֹשֵׂיהֶם כֹּל אֲשֶׁר בֹּטֵחַ בָּהֶם: יִשְׂרָאֵל בְּטַח בַּיהוָה עֶזְרָם וּמָגִנָּם הוּא: בֵּית אַהֲרֹן בִּטְחוּ בַיהוָה עֶזְרָם וּמָגִנָּם הוּא: יִרְאֵי יְהוָה בִּטְחוּ בַיהוָה עֶזְרָם וּמָגִנָּם הוּא:

יְהוָה זְכָרָנוּ יְבָרֵךְ יְבָרֵךְ אֶת בֵּית יִשְׂרָאֵל יְבָרֵךְ אֶת בֵּית אַהֲרֹן: יְבָרֵךְ יִרְאֵי יְהוָה הַקְּטַנִּים עִם הַגְּדֹלִים: יֹסֵף יְהוָה עֲלֵיכֶם עֲלֵיכֶם וְעַל בְּנֵיכֶם: בְּרוּכִים אַתֶּם לַיהוָה עֹשֵׂה שָׁמַיִם וָאָרֶץ: הַשָּׁמַיִם שָׁמַיִם לַיהוָה וְהָאָרֶץ נָתַן לִבְנֵי אָדָם: לֹא הַמֵּתִים יְהַלְלוּ יָהּ וְלֹא כָּל יֹרְדֵי דוּמָה: וַאֲנַחְנוּ נְבָרֵךְ יָהּ מֵעַתָּה וְעַד עוֹלָם הַלְלוּיָהּ:

אָהַבְתִּי כִּי יִשְׁמַע יְהוָה אֶת קוֹלִי תַּחֲנוּנָי: כִּי הִטָּה אָזְנוֹ לִי וּבְיָמַי אֶקְרָא: אֲפָפוּנִי חֶבְלֵי מָוֶת וּמְצָרֵי שְׁאוֹל מְצָאוּנִי צָרָה וְיָגוֹן אֶמְצָא: וּבְשֵׁם יְהוָה אֶקְרָא אָנָּה יְהוָה מַלְּטָה נַפְשִׁי: חַנּוּן יְהוָה וְצַדִּיק וֵאלֹהֵינוּ מְרַחֵם: שֹׁמֵר פְּתָאיִם יְהוָה דַּלּוֹתִי וְלִי יְהוֹשִׁיעַ: שׁוּבִי נַפְשִׁי לִמְנוּחָיְכִי כִּי יְהוָה גָּמַל עָלָיְכִי: כִּי חִלַּצְתָּ נַפְשִׁי מִמָּוֶת אֶת עֵינִי מִן דִּמְעָה אֶת רַגְלִי מִדֶּחִי: אֶתְהַלֵּךְ לִפְנֵי יְהוָה בְּאַרְצוֹת הַחַיִּים: הֶאֱמַנְתִּי

קַדֵּשׁ
KADDESH

וּרְחַץ
URECHATZ

כַּרְפַּס
KARPAS

יַחַץ
YACHATZ

מַגִּיד
MAGGID

רָחְצָה
RACHTZAH

מוֹצִיא
MOTZI

מַצָּה
MATZAH

מָרוֹר
MAROR

כּוֹרֵךְ
KORECH

שֻׁלְחָן עוֹרֵךְ
SHULCHAN ORECH

צָפוּן
TZAFUN

בָּרֵךְ
BARECH

הַלֵּל
HALLEL

נִרְצָה
NIRTZAH

Not for our sake, O Lord, not for our sake, but for Your Name's sake give glory, for the sake of Your kindness and Your truth! Why should the nations say: 'Where is their God?' Our God is in the heavens; whatever He pleases, He does! Their idols are silver and gold, the handiwork of man. They have a mouth, but cannot speak; they have eyes, but cannot see; they have ears, but cannot hear; they have a nose, but cannot smell; their hands — they cannot feel; their feet — they cannot walk; nor can they utter a sound with their throat. Those who make them should become like them, whoever trusts in them! O Israel! Trust in HASHEM — He is their help and shield! House of Aaron! Trust in HASHEM! He is their help and shield. You who fear HASHEM! — trust in HASHEM, He is their help and shield!

The ideas and ideals which distinguish us from the other nations are highlighted as we plead for the future redemption — not for our sake, but to sanctify God's Name.

HASHEM Who has remembered us will bless — He will bless the House of Israel; He will bless the House of Aaron; He will bless those who fear HASHEM, the small as well as the great. May HASHEM add upon you, upon you and your children! You are blessed of HASHEM, maker of heaven and earth. As for the heaven — the heaven is HASHEM's, but the earth He has given to mankind. Neither the dead can praise HASHEM, nor any who descend into silence; but we will bless God henceforth and forever. Halleluyah!

I love Him for HASHEM hears my voice, my supplications. For He has inclined His ear to me, all my days I will call upon Him. The ropes of death encompassed me; the confines of the grave have found me; trouble and sorrow have I found. Then I called upon the Name of HASHEM: 'Please HASHEM, save my soul', Gracious is HASHEM and righteous, our God is merciful. The Lord protects the simple; I was brought low but He saved me. Return to your rest, my soul, for HASHEM has been kind to you. You delivered my soul from death, my eyes from tears and my feet from stumbling. I shall walk before the Lord in the lands of

The recollection of dangers past, overcome through the help of God, endows us with an unshakeable trust in His salvation from our present distress. As we approach the future we are secure in our faith.

65 □ THE FAMILY HAGGADAH

כִּי אֲדַבֵּר אֲנִי עָנִיתִי מְאֹד: אֲנִי אָמַרְתִּי בְחָפְזִי
כָּל הָאָדָם כֹּזֵב:

מָה אָשִׁיב לַיהוה כָּל תַּגְמוּלוֹהִי עָלָי:
כּוֹס יְשׁוּעוֹת אֶשָּׂא וּבְשֵׁם
יהוה אֶקְרָא: נְדָרַי לַיהוה אֲשַׁלֵּם נֶגְדָה נָּא לְכָל
עַמּוֹ: יָקָר בְּעֵינֵי יהוה הַמָּוְתָה לַחֲסִידָיו: אָנָּה
יהוה כִּי אֲנִי עַבְדֶּךָ אֲנִי עַבְדְּךָ בֶּן אֲמָתֶךָ פִּתַּחְתָּ
לְמוֹסֵרָי: לְךָ אֶזְבַּח זֶבַח תּוֹדָה וּבְשֵׁם יהוה
אֶקְרָא: נְדָרַי לַיהוה אֲשַׁלֵּם נֶגְדָה נָּא לְכָל עַמּוֹ:
בְּחַצְרוֹת בֵּית יהוה בְּתוֹכֵכִי יְרוּשָׁלָיִם הַלְלוּיָהּ:

הַלְלוּ אֶת יהוה כָּל גּוֹיִם שַׁבְּחוּהוּ כָּל
הָאֻמִּים: כִּי גָבַר עָלֵינוּ חַסְדּוֹ וֶאֱמֶת
יהוה לְעוֹלָם הַלְלוּיָהּ:

הוֹדוּ לַיהוה כִּי טוֹב   כִּי לְעוֹלָם חַסְדּוֹ:
יֹאמַר נָא יִשְׂרָאֵל   כִּי לְעוֹלָם חַסְדּוֹ:
יֹאמְרוּ נָא בֵית אַהֲרֹן   כִּי לְעוֹלָם חַסְדּוֹ:
יֹאמְרוּ נָא יִרְאֵי יהוה   כִּי לְעוֹלָם חַסְדּוֹ:

מִן הַמֵּצַר קָרָאתִי יָּהּ עָנָנִי בַמֶּרְחָב יָהּ:
יהוה לִי לֹא אִירָא מַה יַּעֲשֶׂה
לִי אָדָם: יהוה לִי בְּעֹזְרָי וַאֲנִי אֶרְאֶה בְשֹׂנְאָי:
טוֹב לַחֲסוֹת בַּיהוה מִבְּטֹחַ בָּאָדָם: טוֹב לַחֲסוֹת
בַּיהוה מִבְּטֹחַ בִּנְדִיבִים: כָּל גּוֹיִם סְבָבוּנִי בְּשֵׁם
יהוה כִּי אֲמִילַם: סַבּוּנִי גַם סְבָבוּנִי בְּשֵׁם יהוה
כִּי אֲמִילַם: סַבּוּנִי כִדְבֹרִים דֹּעֲכוּ כְּאֵשׁ קוֹצִים
בְּשֵׁם יהוה כִּי אֲמִילַם: דָּחֹה דְחִיתַנִי לִנְפֹּל
וַיהוה עֲזָרָנִי: עָזִּי וְזִמְרָת יָהּ וַיְהִי לִי לִישׁוּעָה:
קוֹל רִנָּה וִישׁוּעָה בְּאָהֳלֵי צַדִּיקִים יְמִין יהוה

the living. I kept faith although I say: 'I suffer exceedingly.' I said in my haste: 'All mankind is deceitful.'

How shall we express our thanks? By praising Him with words and deeds. And by praying for His Temple to be rebuilt that we may worship there.

How can I repay HASHEM for all His kindness to me? I will raise the cup of salvations, and invoke the Name of HASHEM. My vows to HASHEM will I pay in the presence of His entire people. Precious in the eyes of HASHEM is the death of His devout ones. Please, HASHEM — for I am Your servant, I am Your servant, son of Your handmaid — You have released my bonds. To You I sacrifice thanksgiving offerings, and the Name of HASHEM will I invoke. My vows to HASHEM will I pay in the presence of His entire people; in the courtyards of the House of HASHEM, in your midst, O Jerusalem. Halleluyah!

The nations are called upon to recognize God and worship Him.

Praise HASHEM, all you nations; praise Him, all you peoples! For His kindness to us was overwhelming, us, and the truth of HASHEM is eternal. Halleluyah!

Not only the Kohanim and the rest of Israel, but all who fear God, must praise Him.

Give thanks to HASHEM for He is good;
      His kindness endures forever!
Let Israel say: His kindness endures forever!
Let the House of Aaron say:
      His kindness endures forever!
Let them who fear HASHEM say:
      His kindness endures forever!

From the straits did I call to God; God answered me with expansiveness. HASHEM is with me, I have no fear; how can man affect me? HASHEM is for me through my helpers; therefore I can face my foes. It is better to take refuge in HASHEM than to rely on man. It is better to take refuge in HASHEM than to rely on princes. All nations encompass me; but in the Name of HASHEM I cut them down. They encompass me. They swarm around me; but in the Name of HASHEM, I cut them down! They swarm around me like bees, but they are extinguished as a fire does thorns; in the Name of HASHEM I cut them down! You pushed me hard that I might fall, but HASHEM assisted me. My strength and song is God; He became my salvation. The sound of rejoicing and salvation is in the tents of the righteous: 'The right hand of HASHEM does

67 ☐ THE FAMILY HAGGADAH

עָשָׂה חָיִל: יְמִין יְהוָה רוֹמֵמָה יְמִין יְהוָה עֹשָׂה
חָיִל: לֹא אָמוּת כִּי אֶחְיֶה וַאֲסַפֵּר מַעֲשֵׂי יָהּ:
יַסֹּר יִסְּרַנִּי יָּהּ וְלַמָּוֶת לֹא נְתָנָנִי: פִּתְחוּ לִי
שַׁעֲרֵי צֶדֶק אָבֹא בָם אוֹדֶה יָהּ: זֶה הַשַּׁעַר
לַיהוָה צַדִּיקִים יָבֹאוּ בוֹ: אוֹדְךָ כִּי עֲנִיתָנִי וַתְּהִי
לִי לִישׁוּעָה: אוֹדְךָ כִּי עֲנִיתָנִי וַתְּהִי לִי לִישׁוּעָה:
אֶבֶן מָאֲסוּ הַבּוֹנִים הָיְתָה לְרֹאשׁ פִּנָּה: אֶבֶן
מָאֲסוּ הַבּוֹנִים הָיְתָה לְרֹאשׁ פִּנָּה: מֵאֵת יְהוָה
הָיְתָה זֹּאת הִיא נִפְלָאת בְּעֵינֵינוּ: מֵאֵת יְהוָה
הָיְתָה זֹּאת הִיא נִפְלָאת בְּעֵינֵינוּ: זֶה הַיּוֹם עָשָׂה
יְהוָה נָגִילָה וְנִשְׂמְחָה בוֹ: זֶה הַיּוֹם עָשָׂה יְהוָה
נָגִילָה וְנִשְׂמְחָה בוֹ:

אָנָּא יְהוָה הוֹשִׁיעָה נָּא:אָנָּא יְהוָה הוֹשִׁיעָה נָּא:
אָנָּא יְהוָה הַצְלִיחָה נָא:אָנָּא יְהוָה הַצְלִיחָה נָא:

בָּרוּךְ הַבָּא בְּשֵׁם יְהוָה בֵּרַכְנוּכֶם מִבֵּית
יְהוָה: בָּרוּךְ הַבָּא בְּשֵׁם יְהוָה
בֵּרַכְנוּכֶם מִבֵּית יְהוָה: אֵל יְהוָה וַיָּאֶר לָנוּ אִסְרוּ
חַג בַּעֲבֹתִים עַד קַרְנוֹת הַמִּזְבֵּחַ: אֵל יְהוָה וַיָּאֶר
לָנוּ אִסְרוּ חַג בַּעֲבֹתִים עַד קַרְנוֹת הַמִּזְבֵּחַ: אֵלִי
אַתָּה וְאוֹדֶךָּ אֱלֹהַי אֲרוֹמְמֶךָּ: אֵלִי אַתָּה וְאוֹדֶךָּ
אֱלֹהַי אֲרוֹמְמֶךָּ: הוֹדוּ לַיהוָה כִּי טוֹב כִּי לְעוֹלָם
חַסְדּוֹ: הוֹדוּ לַיהוָה כִּי טוֹב כִּי לְעוֹלָם חַסְדּוֹ:

יְהַלְלוּךְ יְהוָה אֱלֹהֵינוּ כָּל מַעֲשֶׂיךָ
וַחֲסִידֶיךָ צַדִּיקִים עוֹשֵׂי רְצוֹנֶךָ
וְכָל עַמְּךָ בֵּית יִשְׂרָאֵל בְּרִנָּה יוֹדוּ וִיבָרְכוּ
וִישַׁבְּחוּ וִיפָאֲרוּ וִירוֹמְמוּ וְיַעֲרִיצוּ וְיַקְדִּישׁוּ
וְיַמְלִיכוּ אֶת שִׁמְךָ מַלְכֵּנוּ כִּי לְךָ טוֹב לְהוֹדוֹת
וּלְשִׁמְךָ נָאֶה לְזַמֵּר כִּי מֵעוֹלָם עַד עוֹלָם אַתָּה
אֵל:

קַדֵּשׁ KADDESH

וּרְחַץ URECHATZ

כַּרְפַּס KARPAS

יַחַץ YACHATZ

מַגִּיד MAGGID

רָחְצָה RACHTZAH

מוֹצִיא MOTZI

מַצָּה MATZAH

מָרוֹר MAROR

כּוֹרֵךְ KORECH

שֻׁלְחָן עוֹרֵךְ SHULCHAN ORECH

צָפוּן TZAFUN

בָּרֵךְ BARECH

הַלֵּל HALLEL

נִרְצָה NIRTZAH

"I shall not die," that is, I shall not act like the wicked who, devoid of positive contribution to this world, are considered as dead, even during their lifetime. "I shall live," in a meaningful way, by serving God.

valiantly! The right hand of HASHEM is raised triumphantly! The right hand of HASHEM does valiantly!' I shall not die! I shall live and relate the deeds of God. God chastened me exceedingly but He did not let me die. Open for me the gates of righteousness, I will enter them and thank God. This is the gate of HASHEM; the righteous shall enter through it. I thank You for You answered me and became my salvation! I thank You for You answered me and became my salvation! The stone which the builders despised has become the cornerstone! The stone which the builders despised has become the cornerstone! This has emanated from HASHEM; it is wondrous in our eyes! This has emanated from HASHEM; it is wondrous in our eyes! This is the day HASHEM has made; we will rejoice and be glad in Him! This is the day HASHEM has made; we will rejoice and be glad in Him!

O HASHEM, please save us!
O HASHEM, please save us!
O HASHEM, please make us prosper!
O HASHEM, please make us prosper!

B lessed be he who comes, in the Name of HASHEM; we bless you from the House of HASHEM. Blessed be he who comes, in the Name of HASHEM; we bless you from the House of HASHEM. HASHEM is God and He illuminated for us; bind the festival offering with cords to the corners of the altar. HASHEM is God and He illuminated for us; bind the festival offering with cords to the corners of the altar. You are my God and I shall thank You; my God and I shall exalt You. You are my God and I shall thank You; my God and shall I exalt You. Give thanks to HASHEM, for He is good; His kindness endures forever! Give thanks to HASHEM, for He is good; His kindness endures forever!

T hey shall praise You, HASHEM our God for all Your works, along with Your pious followers, the righteous, who do Your will, and Your entire people, the House of Israel, with joy will thank, bless, praise, glorify, exalt, revere, sanctify, and coronate Your name, our King! For to You it is fitting to give thanks, and unto Your name it is proper to sing praises, for from eternity to eternity You are God.

הוֹדוּ לַיהוה כִּי טוֹב   כִּי לְעוֹלָם חַסְדּוֹ:
הוֹדוּ לֵאלֹהֵי הָאֱלֹהִים   כִּי לְעוֹלָם חַסְדּוֹ:
הוֹדוּ לַאֲדֹנֵי הָאֲדֹנִים   כִּי לְעוֹלָם חַסְדּוֹ:
לְעֹשֵׂה נִפְלָאוֹת גְּדֹלוֹת לְבַדּוֹ כִּי לְעוֹלָם חַסְדּוֹ:
לְעֹשֵׂה הַשָּׁמַיִם בִּתְבוּנָה   כִּי לְעוֹלָם חַסְדּוֹ:
לְרֹקַע הָאָרֶץ עַל הַמָּיִם   כִּי לְעוֹלָם חַסְדּוֹ:
לְעֹשֵׂה אוֹרִים גְּדֹלִים   כִּי לְעוֹלָם חַסְדּוֹ:
אֶת הַשֶּׁמֶשׁ לְמֶמְשֶׁלֶת בַּיּוֹם כִּי לְעוֹלָם חַסְדּוֹ:
אֶת הַיָּרֵחַ וְכוֹכָבִים
לְמֶמְשְׁלוֹת בַּלַּיְלָה   כִּי לְעוֹלָם חַסְדּוֹ:
לְמַכֵּה מִצְרַיִם בִּבְכוֹרֵיהֶם   כִּי לְעוֹלָם חַסְדּוֹ:
וַיּוֹצֵא יִשְׂרָאֵל מִתּוֹכָם   כִּי לְעוֹלָם חַסְדּוֹ:
בְּיָד חֲזָקָה וּבִזְרוֹעַ נְטוּיָה   כִּי לְעוֹלָם חַסְדּוֹ:
לְגֹזֵר יַם סוּף לִגְזָרִים   כִּי לְעוֹלָם חַסְדּוֹ:
וְהֶעֱבִיר יִשְׂרָאֵל בְּתוֹכוֹ   כִּי לְעוֹלָם חַסְדּוֹ:
וְנִעֵר פַּרְעֹה וְחֵילוֹ בְיַם סוּף כִּי לְעוֹלָם חַסְדּוֹ:
לְמוֹלִיךְ עַמּוֹ בַּמִּדְבָּר   כִּי לְעוֹלָם חַסְדּוֹ:
לְמַכֵּה מְלָכִים גְּדֹלִים   כִּי לְעוֹלָם חַסְדּוֹ:
וַיַּהֲרֹג מְלָכִים אַדִּירִים   כִּי לְעוֹלָם חַסְדּוֹ:
לְסִיחוֹן מֶלֶךְ הָאֱמֹרִי   כִּי לְעוֹלָם חַסְדּוֹ:
וּלְעוֹג מֶלֶךְ הַבָּשָׁן   כִּי לְעוֹלָם חַסְדּוֹ:
וְנָתַן אַרְצָם לְנַחֲלָה   כִּי לְעוֹלָם חַסְדּוֹ:
נַחֲלָה לְיִשְׂרָאֵל עַבְדּוֹ   כִּי לְעוֹלָם חַסְדּוֹ:
שֶׁבְּשִׁפְלֵנוּ זָכַר לָנוּ   כִּי לְעוֹלָם חַסְדּוֹ:
וַיִּפְרְקֵנוּ מִצָּרֵינוּ   כִּי לְעוֹלָם חַסְדּוֹ:
נֹתֵן לֶחֶם לְכָל בָּשָׂר   כִּי לְעוֹלָם חַסְדּוֹ:
הוֹדוּ לְאֵל הַשָּׁמָיִם   כִּי לְעוֹלָם חַסְדּוֹ:

נִשְׁמַת כָּל חַי תְּבָרֵךְ אֶת שִׁמְךָ יהוה
אֱלֹהֵינוּ וְרוּחַ כָּל בָּשָׂר תְּפָאֵר

קַדֵּשׁ
KADDESH

וּרְחַץ
URECHATZ

כַּרְפַּס
KARPAS

יַחַץ
YACHATZ

מַגִּיד
MAGGID

רָחְצָה
RACHTZAH

מוֹצִיא
MOTZI

מַצָּה
MATZAH

מָרוֹר
MAROR

כּוֹרֵךְ
KORECH

שֻׁלְחָן
עוֹרֵךְ
SHULCHAN
ORECH

צָפוּן
TZAFUN

בָּרֵךְ
BARECH

הַלֵּל
HALLEL

נִרְצָה
NIRTZAH

70 ☐ הגדה של פסח

Give thanks to HASHEM, for He is good;

His kindness endures forever!

Give thanks to the God of gods;   His kindness endures forever!

Give thanks to the Master of masters;

His kindness endures forever!

To Him Who alone does great wonders;

His kindness endures forever!

To Him Who made the heaven with understanding;

His kindness endures forever!

To Him Who stretched out the earth over the waters;

His kindness endures forever!

To Him Who made great luminaries;

His kindness endures forever!

The sun for the reign of day;   His kindness endures forever!

In twenty-six The moon and the stars for the reign of night;

verses,

representing the His kindness endures forever!

twenty-six To Him Who struck the Egyptians through their firstborn;

generations from

Creation until the His kindness endures forever!

Exodus and the And removed Israel from their midst;

giving of the Torah,

the Psalmist His kindness endures forever!

recapitulates the With strong hand and outstretched arm;

history of the world

up to the Israelites' His kindness endures forever!

entry into the Holy Who divided the Sea of Reeds into parts;

Land. For each

occurrence we His kindness endures forever!

thank God for his And caused Israel to pass through it;

enduring kindness.

His kindness endures forever!

And threw Pharaoh and his army into the Sea of Reeds;

His kindness endures forever!

To Him Who led His people through the wilderness;

His kindness endures forever!

To Him Who smote great kings;   His kindness endures forever!

And slew mighty kings;   His kindness endures forever!

Sichon, king of the Emorites;   His kindness endures forever!

And Og, king of Bashan;   His kindness endures forever!

And gave their land as an inheritance;

His kindness endures forever!

An inheritance to Israel His servant; His kindness endures forever!

Who remembered us in our lowliness;

His kindness endures forever!

And released us from our foes;   His kindness endures forever!

He gives food to all living creatures; His kindness endures forever!

Give thanks to God of heaven;   His kindness endures forever!

The soul of every living being shall bless Your Name,
HASHEM our God; the spirit of all flesh shall always

71 □ THE FAMILY HAGGADAH

וּתְרוֹמֵם זִכְרְךָ מַלְכֵּנוּ תָּמִיד. מִן הָעוֹלָם וְעַד
הָעוֹלָם אַתָּה אֵל וּמִבַּלְעָדֶיךָ אֵין לָנוּ מֶלֶךְ גּוֹאֵל
וּמוֹשִׁיעַ פּוֹדֶה וּמַצִּיל וּמְפַרְנֵס וּמְרַחֵם בְּכָל עֵת
צָרָה וְצוּקָה. אֵין לָנוּ מֶלֶךְ אֶלָּא אָתָּה. אֱלֹהֵי
הָרִאשׁוֹנִים וְהָאַחֲרוֹנִים אֱלוֹהַּ כָּל בְּרִיּוֹת אֲדוֹן
כָּל תּוֹלָדוֹת הַמְהֻלָּל בְּרֹב הַתִּשְׁבָּחוֹת הַמְנַהֵג
עוֹלָמוֹ בְּחֶסֶד וּבְרִיּוֹתָיו בְּרַחֲמִים וַיהוה לֹא יָנוּם
וְלֹא יִישָׁן הַמְעוֹרֵר יְשֵׁנִים וְהַמֵּקִיץ נִרְדָּמִים
וְהַמֵּשִׂיחַ אִלְּמִים וְהַמַּתִּיר אֲסוּרִים וְהַסּוֹמֵךְ
נוֹפְלִים וְהַזּוֹקֵף כְּפוּפִים לְךָ לְבַדְּךָ אֲנַחְנוּ
מוֹדִים. אִלּוּ פִינוּ מָלֵא שִׁירָה כַּיָּם וּלְשׁוֹנֵנוּ רִנָּה
כַּהֲמוֹן גַּלָּיו וְשִׂפְתוֹתֵינוּ שֶׁבַח כְּמֶרְחֲבֵי רָקִיעַ
וְעֵינֵינוּ מְאִירוֹת כַּשֶּׁמֶשׁ וְכַיָּרֵחַ וְיָדֵינוּ פְרוּשׂוֹת
כְּנִשְׁרֵי שָׁמָיִם וְרַגְלֵינוּ קַלּוֹת כָּאַיָּלוֹת אֵין אֲנַחְנוּ
מַסְפִּיקִים לְהוֹדוֹת לְךָ יהוה אֱלֹהֵינוּ וֵאלֹהֵי
אֲבוֹתֵינוּ וּלְבָרֵךְ אֶת שְׁמֶךָ עַל אַחַת מֵאֶלֶף
אַלְפֵי אֲלָפִים וְרִבֵּי רְבָבוֹת פְּעָמִים הַטּוֹבוֹת
שֶׁעָשִׂיתָ עִם אֲבוֹתֵינוּ וְעִמָּנוּ. מִמִּצְרַיִם גְּאַלְתָּנוּ
יהוה אֱלֹהֵינוּ וּמִבֵּית עֲבָדִים פְּדִיתָנוּ בְּרָעָב
זַנְתָּנוּ וּבְשָׂבָע כִּלְכַּלְתָּנוּ מֵחֶרֶב הִצַּלְתָּנוּ וּמִדֶּבֶר
מִלַּטְתָּנוּ וּמֵחֳלָיִם רָעִים וְנֶאֱמָנִים דִּלִּיתָנוּ. עַד
הֵנָּה עֲזָרוּנוּ רַחֲמֶיךָ וְלֹא עֲזָבוּנוּ חֲסָדֶיךָ וְאַל
תִּטְּשֵׁנוּ יהוה אֱלֹהֵינוּ לָנֶצַח. עַל כֵּן אֵבָרִים
שֶׁפִּלַּגְתָּ בָּנוּ וְרוּחַ וּנְשָׁמָה שֶׁנָּפַחְתָּ בְּאַפֵּינוּ
וְלָשׁוֹן אֲשֶׁר שַׂמְתָּ בְּפִינוּ הֵן הֵם יוֹדוּ וִיבָרְכוּ
וִישַׁבְּחוּ וִיפָאֲרוּ וִירוֹמְמוּ וְיַעֲרִיצוּ וְיַקְדִּישׁוּ
וְיַמְלִיכוּ אֶת שִׁמְךָ מַלְכֵּנוּ. כִּי כָל פֶּה לְךָ יוֹדֶה
וְכָל לָשׁוֹן לְךָ תִשָּׁבַע וְכָל בֶּרֶךְ לְךָ תִכְרַע וְכָל
קוֹמָה לְפָנֶיךָ תִשְׁתַּחֲוֶה וְכָל לְבָבוֹת יִירָאוּךָ וְכָל

קַדֵּשׁ
KADDESH

וּרְחַץ
URECHATZ

כַּרְפַּס
KARPAS

יַחַץ
YACHATZ

מַגִּיד
MAGGID

רָחְצָה
RACHTZAH

מוֹצִיא
MOTZI

מַצָּה
MATZAH

מָרוֹר
MAROR

כּוֹרֵךְ
KORECH

שֻׁלְחָן
עוֹרֵךְ
SHULCHAN
ORECH

צָפוּן
TZAFUN

בָּרֵךְ
BARECH

הַלֵּל
HALLEL

נִרְצָה
NIRTZAH

glorify and exalt Your remembrance, our King. From eternity to eternity, You are God, and except for You we have no king, redeemer or helper. O Rescuer, and Redeemer, Sustainer and Merciful One in every time of trouble and distress. We have no King but You — God of the first and of the last, God of all creatures, Master of all generations, Who is extolled through a multitude of praises, Who guides His world with kindness and His creatures with mercy. HASHEM neither slumbers nor sleeps; He rouses the sleepers and awakens the slumbers; He makes the mute speak and frees the bound; He supports the falling and raises erect the bowed down. To You alone we give thanks.

We praise and thank God for His universal beneficence; He is the First, He is the Last; He is Eternal — God of all creatures, of all generations, of all humanity. But in the last analysis we acknowledge our allegiance to Him, not because we understand His achievements, but for Himself alone. His greatness, not merely His largesse, is the source of our adoration and love for Him.

Were our mouths as full of song as the sea, and our tongue as full of jubilation as its multitudes of waves, and our lips as full of praise as the breadth of the heavens, and our eyes as brilliant as the sun and the moon, and our hands as outspread in prayer as the eagles of the sky and our feet as swift as deer — we still could not sufficiently thank You, HASHEM our God and God of our fathers, and bless Your Name, for even one of the thousands upon thousands and myriads upon myriads of favors, miracles and wonders, which You performed for our fathers and for us. You liberated us from Egypt, HASHEM our God, and redeemed us from the house of bondage. In famine You nourished us and in plenty You supported us. From the sword You saved us; from the plague You let us escape; and You spared us from severe and enduring diseases. Until now Your mercy has helped us, and Your kindness has not forsaken us. Do not abandon us, HASHEM our God, to the ultimate end.

Therefore, the limbs which You set within us, and the spirit and soul which You breathed into our nostrils, and the tongue which You have placed in our mouth — they shall all thank and bless, praise and glorify, exalt, be devoted to, sanctify and do homage to Your Name, our King forever. For every mouth shall offer thanks to You; every tongue shall vow allegiance to You; every knee shall bend to You; all who stand erect shall bow before You; all hearts shall fear You; and

73 □ THE FAMILY HAGGADAH

קֶרֶב וּכְלָיוֹת יְזַמְּרוּ לִשְׁמֶךָ. כַּדָּבָר שֶׁכָּתוּב כָּל עַצְמֹתַי תֹּאמַרְנָה יהוה מִי כָמֽוֹךָ מַצִּיל עָנִי מֵחָזָק מִמֶּֽנּוּ וְעָנִי וְאֶבְיוֹן מִגֹּזְלוֹ. מִי יִדְמֶה לָךְ וּמִי יִשְׁוֶה לָּךְ וּמִי יַעֲרָךְ לָךְ הָאֵל הַגָּדוֹל הַגִּבּוֹר וְהַנּוֹרָא אֵל עֶלְיוֹן קֹנֵה שָׁמַֽיִם וָאָֽרֶץ. נְהַלֶּלְךָ וּנְשַׁבֵּחֲךָ וּנְפָאֶרְךָ וּנְבָרֵךְ אֶת שֵׁם קָדְשֶֽׁךָ כָּאָמוּר לְדָוִד בָּרְכִי נַפְשִׁי אֶת יהוה וְכָל קְרָבַי אֶת שֵׁם קָדְשׁוֹ:

הָאֵל בְּתַעֲצֻמוֹת עֻזֶּךָ הַגָּדוֹל בִּכְבוֹד שְׁמֶךָ הַגִּבּוֹר לָנֶֽצַח וְהַנּוֹרָא בְּנוֹרְאוֹתֶֽיךָ הַמֶּֽלֶךְ הַיּוֹשֵׁב עַל כִּסֵּא רָם וְנִשָּׂא:

שׁוֹכֵן עַד מָרוֹם וְקָדוֹשׁ שְׁמוֹ. וְכָתוּב רַנְּנוּ צַדִּיקִים בַּיהוה לַיְשָׁרִים נָאוָה תְהִלָּה: בְּפִי יְשָׁרִים תִּתְהַלָּל וּבְדִבְרֵי צַדִּיקִים תִּתְבָּרַךְ וּבִלְשׁוֹן חֲסִידִים תִּתְרוֹמָם וּבְקֶֽרֶב קְדוֹשִׁים תִּתְקַדָּשׁ:

וּבְמַקְהֲלוֹת רִבְבוֹת עַמְּךָ בֵּית יִשְׂרָאֵל בְּרִנָּה יִתְפָּאֵר שִׁמְךָ מַלְכֵּֽנוּ בְּכָל דּוֹר וָדוֹר שֶׁכֵּן חוֹבַת כָּל הַיְצוּרִים לְפָנֶֽיךָ יהוה אֱלֹהֵֽינוּ וֵאלֹהֵי אֲבוֹתֵֽינוּ לְהוֹדוֹת לְהַלֵּל לְשַׁבֵּֽחַ לְפָאֵר לְרוֹמֵם לְהַדֵּר לְבָרֵךְ לְעַלֵּה וּלְקַלֵּס עַל כָּל דִּבְרֵי שִׁירוֹת וְתִשְׁבְּחוֹת דָּוִד בֶּן יִשַׁי עַבְדְּךָ מְשִׁיחֶֽךָ:

יִשְׁתַּבַּח שִׁמְךָ לָעַד מַלְכֵּֽנוּ הָאֵל הַמֶּֽלֶךְ הַגָּדוֹל וְהַקָּדוֹשׁ בַּשָּׁמַֽיִם וּבָאָֽרֶץ כִּי לְךָ נָאֶה יהוה אֱלֹהֵֽינוּ וֵאלֹהֵי אֲבוֹתֵֽינוּ שִׁיר וּשְׁבָחָה הַלֵּל וְזִמְרָה עֹז וּמֶמְשָׁלָה נֶֽצַח גְּדֻלָּה וּגְבוּרָה תְּהִלָּה וְתִפְאֶֽרֶת קְדֻשָּׁה וּמַלְכוּת

74 □ הגדה של פסח

men's innermost feelings and thoughts shall sing praises to Your name, as it is written (Psalms 35:10): All my bones shall say:'HASHEM, who is like You?' You save the poor man from one stronger than him, the poor and needy from one who would rob him. Who may be likened to You? Who is equal to You? Who can be compared to You? O great, mighty, and awesome God, supreme God, Maker of heaven and earth. We shall praise, acclaim, and glorify You and bless Your holy Name, as it is said (Psalms 103:1): A Psalm of David: Bless HASHEM, O my soul, and let my whole inner being bless His holy Name!

O God in the omnipotence of Your strength, great in the honor of Your name, powerful forever and awesome through Your awesome deeds, O King enthroned upon a high and lofty throne!

He Who abides forever, exalted and holy is His Name. And it is written (Psalms 33:1): Rejoice in HASHEM, you righteous; for the upright His praise is pleasant. By the mouth of the upright You shall be praised; by the words of the righteous You shall be blessed; by the tongue of the pious You shall be exalted; and amid the holy You shall be sanctified.

And in the assemblies of the myriads of Your people, the House of Israel, with jubilation shall Your name, our King, be glorified in every generation. For such is the duty of all creatures — before You, HASHEM, our God and God of our fathers, to thank, praise, laud, glorify, exalt, adore, bless, raise high, and sing praises — even beyond all expressions of the songs and praises of David the son of Jesse, Your servant, Your anointed.

May Your Name be praised forever, our King, the God and King Who is great and holy in heaven and on earth; for to You, HASHEM our God and God of our fathers, it is fitting to render song and praise, hallel and hymns, power and dominion, victory, greatness and might, praise and glory, holiness and sovereignty,

75 □ THE FAMILY HAGGADAH

בְּרָכוֹת וְהוֹדָאוֹת מֵעַתָּה וְעַד עוֹלָם: בָּרוּךְ אַתָּה
יהוה אֵל מֶלֶךְ גָּדוֹל בַּתִּשְׁבָּחוֹת אֵל הַהוֹדָאוֹת
אֲדוֹן הַנִּפְלָאוֹת הַבּוֹחֵר בְּשִׁירֵי זִמְרָה מֶלֶךְ אֵל
חֵי הָעוֹלָמִים:

*The blessing over wine is recited and the fourth cup is drunk while reclining
to the left side. It is preferable that the entire cup be drunk.*

בָּרוּךְ אַתָּה יהוה אֱלֹהֵינוּ מֶלֶךְ הָעוֹלָם
בּוֹרֵא פְּרִי הַגָּפֶן:

*After drinking the fourth cup, the concluding blessing is recited.
On the Sabbath include the passage in parentheses.*

בָּרוּךְ אַתָּה יהוה אֱלֹהֵינוּ מֶלֶךְ הָעוֹלָם עַל
הַגֶּפֶן וְעַל פְּרִי הַגֶּפֶן וְעַל תְּנוּבַת
הַשָּׂדֶה וְעַל אֶרֶץ חֶמְדָּה טוֹבָה וּרְחָבָה שֶׁרָצִיתָ
וְהִנְחַלְתָּ לַאֲבוֹתֵינוּ לֶאֱכֹל מִפִּרְיָהּ וְלִשְׂבֹּעַ
מִטּוּבָהּ. רַחֵם נָא יהוה אֱלֹהֵינוּ עַל יִשְׂרָאֵל עַמֶּךְ
וְעַל יְרוּשָׁלַיִם עִירֶךְ וְעַל צִיּוֹן מִשְׁכַּן כְּבוֹדֶךְ וְעַל
מִזְבַּחֶךְ וְעַל הֵיכָלֶךְ וּבְנֵה יְרוּשָׁלַיִם עִיר הַקֹּדֶשׁ
בִּמְהֵרָה בְיָמֵינוּ וְהַעֲלֵנוּ לְתוֹכָהּ וְשַׂמְּחֵנוּ
בְּבִנְיָנָהּ וְנֹאכַל מִפִּרְיָהּ וְנִשְׂבַּע מִטּוּבָהּ וּנְבָרֶכְךָ
עָלֶיהָ בִּקְדֻשָּׁה וּבְטָהֳרָה (וּרְצֵה וְהַחֲלִיצֵנוּ בְּיוֹם
הַשַּׁבָּת הַזֶּה) וְשַׂמְּחֵנוּ בְּיוֹם חַג הַמַּצּוֹת הַזֶּה כִּי
אַתָּה יהוה טוֹב וּמֵטִיב לַכֹּל וְנוֹדֶה לְּךָ עַל
הָאָרֶץ וְעַל פְּרִי הַגָּפֶן: בָּרוּךְ אַתָּה יהוה עַל
הָאָרֶץ וְעַל פְּרִי הַגָּפֶן:

חֲסַל סִדּוּר פֶּסַח כְּהִלְכָתוֹ. כְּכָל מִשְׁפָּטוֹ
וְחֻקָּתוֹ. כַּאֲשֶׁר זָכִינוּ לְסַדֵּר אוֹתוֹ. כֵּן
נִזְכֶּה לַעֲשׂוֹתוֹ: זָךְ שׁוֹכֵן מְעוֹנָה. קוֹמֵם קְהַל

blessings and thanksgiving, from now and forever. Blessed are You, HASHEM, God, King, great in praises, God of thanksgiving, Master of wonders, Who favors songs of praise — King, God, Life of all worlds.

The blessing over wine is recited and the fourth cup is drunk while reclining to the left side. It is preferable that the entire cup be drunk.

Blessed are You, HASHEM our God, King of the universe, Who creates the fruit of the vine.

After drinking the fourth cup, the concluding blessing is recited. On the Sabbath include the passage in parentheses.

Blessed are You, HASHEM our God, King of the universe, for the vine and the fruit of the vine, and for the produce of the field. For the desirable, good, and spacious land that You were pleased to give our forefathers as a heritage, to eat of its fruit and to be satisfied with its goodness. Have mercy, we beg You, HASHEM our God, on Israel Your people; on Jerusalem, Your city; on Zion, resting place of Your glory; Your altar, and Your Temple. Rebuild Jerusalem the city of holiness, speedily in our days. Bring us up into it and gladden us in its rebuilding and let us eat from its fruit and be satisfied with its goodness and bless You upon it in holiness and purity. (Favor us and strengthen us on this Sabbath day) and grant us happiness on this Festival of Matzos; for You, HASHEM, are good and do good to all, and we thank You for the land and for the fruit of the vine. Blessed are You, HASHEM, for the land and for the fruit of the vine.

In accordance with the verse, "Let my tongue adhere to my palate ... if I fail to elevate Jerusalem above my foremost joy!" we pray that our reenactment of the past redemption set the stage for the future redemption, that we may celebrate next year's Seder in the Holy City.

NIRTZAH

The Seder is now concluded in accordance with its laws, with all its ordinances and statutes. Just as we were privileged to arrange it, so may we merit to perform it. O Pure One, Who dwells on high, raise up the

עֲדַת מִי מָנָה. בְּקָרוֹב נַהֵל נִטְעֵי כַנָּה. פְּדוּיִם
לְצִיּוֹן בְּרִנָּה:

לְשָׁנָה הַבָּאָה בִּירוּשָׁלָיִם:

On the first night recite the following.
On the second night continue on page 80.

וּבְכֵן וַיְהִי בַּחֲצִי הַלַּיְלָה:

בַּלַּיְלָה.	אָז רוֹב נִסִּים הִפְלֵאתָ
הַלַּיְלָה.	בְּרֹאשׁ אַשְׁמוֹרֶת זֶה
לַיְלָה.	גֵּר צֶדֶק נִצַּחְתּוֹ כְּנֶחֱלַק לוֹ

וַיְהִי בַּחֲצִי הַלַּיְלָה:

הַלַּיְלָה.	דַּנְתָּ מֶלֶךְ גְּרָר בַּחֲלוֹם
לַיְלָה.	הִפְחַדְתָּ אֲרַמִּי בְּאֶמֶשׁ
לַיְלָה.	וַיָּשַׂר יִשְׂרָאֵל לְמַלְאָךְ וַיּוּכַל לוֹ

וַיְהִי בַּחֲצִי הַלַּיְלָה:

הַלַּיְלָה.	זֶרַע בְּכוֹרֵי פַתְרוֹס מָחַצְתָּ בַּחֲצִי
בַּלַּיְלָה.	חֵילָם לֹא מָצְאוּ בְּקוּמָם
לַיְלָה.	טִיסַת נְגִיד חֲרֹשֶׁת סִלִּיתָ בְּכוֹכְבֵי

וַיְהִי בַּחֲצִי הַלַּיְלָה:

יָעַץ מְחָרֵף לְנוֹפֵף אִוּוּי הוֹבַשְׁתָּ פְּגָרָיו בַּלַּיְלָה.	
לַיְלָה.	כָּרַע בֵּל וּמַצָּבוֹ בְּאִישׁוֹן
לַיְלָה.	לְאִישׁ חֲמוּדוֹת נִגְלָה רָז חֲזוֹת

וַיְהִי בַּחֲצִי הַלַּיְלָה:

בַּלַּיְלָה.	מִשְׁתַּכֵּר בִּכְלֵי קֹדֶשׁ נֶהֱרַג בּוֹ
לַיְלָה.	נוֹשַׁע מִבּוֹר אֲרָיוֹת פּוֹתֵר בְּעִתּוּתֵי
בַּלַּיְלָה.	שִׂנְאָה נָטַר אֲגָגִי וְכָתַב סְפָרִים

וַיְהִי בַּחֲצִי הַלַּיְלָה:

לַיְלָה.	עוֹרַרְתָּ נִצְחֲךָ עָלָיו בְּנֶדֶד שְׁנַת

countless congregation, soon — guide the offshoots
of Your plants, redeemed, to Zion with glad song.

NEXT YEAR IN JERUSALEM

On the first night recite the following.
On the second night continue on page 80.

It came to pass at midnight.

You performed many miracles in the past at night: Abraham defeated the four kings; Abimelech was judged for kidnapping Sarah; Laban was warned, in a dream, not to harm Jacob; Jacob defeated Esau's guardian angel; the Egyptian firstborn died and their wealth was lost; Sisera's army was destroyed; Sennacherib and his armies fell dead; Nebuchadnezzar's statue and its pedestal broke; Daniel interpreted Nebuchadnezzar's dreams; Belshazzar was killed just after Daniel disclosed the secret of "the handwriting on the wall"; and Ahasuerus' sleep was disturbed, leading to Haman's downfall.

You have, of old, performed many wonders by night.
At the head of the watches of   this night.
To the righteous convert (Abraham),
     You gave triumph by dividing for him   the night.
         It came to pass at midnight.
You judged the king of Gerar (Abimelech), in a dream
                by night.
You frightened the Aramean (Laban), in the dark
                of night.
Israel (Jacob) fought with an angel and overcame him
                by night.
         It came to pass at midnight.
Egypt's first-born You crushed at   midnight.
Their host they found not upon arising at   night.
The army of the prince of Charoshes (Sisera)
     You swept away with stars of   the night.
         It came to pass at midnight.
The blasphemer (Sennacherib), planned to raise his
    hand against Jerusalem—
but You withered his corpses   by night.
Bel was overturned with its pedestal, in the darkness
                of night.
To the man of Your delights (Daniel),
    was revealed the mystery of the visions   of night.
         It came to pass at midnight.
He (Belshazzar) who caroused from the holy vessels
    was killed that very   night.
From the lions' den was rescued he (Daniel)
    who interpreted the 'terrors' of   the night.
The Aggagite (Haman) nursed hatred
    and wrote decrees   at night.
         It came to pass at midnight.
You began Your triumph over him
    when You disturbed (Ahasuerus') sleep   at night.

79 □ THE FAMILY HAGGADAH

	פּוּרָה תִדְרוֹךְ לְשׁמֵר מַה	מִלַּיְלָה.
	צָרַח כַּשֹּׁמֵר וְשָׂח אָתָא בֹקֶר וְגַם	לַיְלָה.
	וַיְהִי בַּחֲצִי הַלַּיְלָה:	

	קָרֵב יוֹם אֲשֶׁר הוּא לֹא יוֹם וְלֹא	לַיְלָה.
	רָם הוֹדַע כִּי לְךָ הַיּוֹם אַף לְךָ	הַלַּיְלָה.
	שׁוֹמְרִים הַפְקֵד לְעִירְךָ כָּל הַיּוֹם וְכָל	הַלַּיְלָה.
	תָּאִיר כְּאוֹר יוֹם חֶשְׁכַּת	לַיְלָה.
	וַיְהִי בַּחֲצִי הַלַּיְלָה:	

On the second night recite the following.
On the first night continue on page 82.

וּבְכֵן וַאֲמַרְתֶּם זֶבַח פֶּסַח:

	אֹמֶץ גְּבוּרוֹתֶיךָ הִפְלֵאתָ	בַּפֶּסַח.
	בְּרֹאשׁ כָּל מוֹעֲדוֹת נִשֵּׂאתָ	פֶּסַח.
	גִּלִּיתָ לְאֶזְרָחִי חֲצוֹת לֵיל	פֶּסַח.
	וַאֲמַרְתֶּם זֶבַח פֶּסַח:	

	דְּלָתָיו דָּפַקְתָּ כְּחֹם הַיּוֹם	בַּפֶּסַח.
	הִסְעִיד נוֹצְצִים עֻגוֹת מַצּוֹת	בַּפֶּסַח.
	וְאֶל הַבָּקָר רָץ זֵכֶר לְשׁוֹר עֵרֶךְ	פֶּסַח.
	וַאֲמַרְתֶּם זֶבַח פֶּסַח:	

	זֹעֲמוּ סְדוֹמִים וְלוֹהֲטוּ בָּאֵשׁ	בַּפֶּסַח.
	חֻלַּץ לוֹט מֵהֶם וּמַצּוֹת אָפָה בְּקֵץ	פֶּסַח.
	טִאטֵאתָ אַדְמַת מוֹף וְנוֹף בְּעָבְרְךָ	בַּפֶּסַח.
	וַאֲמַרְתֶּם זֶבַח פֶּסַח:	

	יָהּ רֹאשׁ כָּל אוֹן מָחַצְתָּ בְּלֵיל שִׁמּוּר	פֶּסַח.
	כַּבִּיר עַל בֵּן בְּכוֹר פָּסַחְתָּ בְּדַם	פֶּסַח.
	לְבִלְתִּי תֵּת מַשְׁחִית לָבֹא בִּפְתָחַי	בַּפֶּסַח.
	וַאֲמַרְתֶּם זֶבַח פֶּסַח:	

"But what will be the outcome of this long exile night?" May You tread on those who oppress us. May light shine for the righteous, and darkness enshroud the wicked. Hasten the time of redemption for Your nation, for Your city. Let the darkness of exile be brightened by the light of day.

Trample the wine-press to help those who ask the
watchman, 'What of the   long night?'
He will shout, like a watchman, and say:
'Morning shall come   after night.'
            It came to pass at midnight.
Hasten the day (of Messiah), that is neither day
                                                            nor night.
Most High — make known that Yours are day
                                                            and night.
Appoint guards for Your city, all the day and all
                                                            the night
Brighten like the light of day the darkness   of night.
            It came to pass at midnight.

On the second night recite the following.
On the first night continue on page 82.

And You shall say: This is the feast of Passover.

You displayed wondrously Your mighty powers
                                                            on Passover.
Above all festivals You elevated   Passover.
To the Oriental (Abraham) You revealed
      the future midnight   of Passover.
      And you shall say: This is the feast of Passover.

Many times have You exhibited Your awesome might on Pesach: You visited Abraham and foretold Isaac's birth; overturned Sodom but saved Lot; granted Joshua victory over Jericho; and delivered Midian into Gideon's hands. Additionally, the defeats of Sennacherib, Belshazzar and Haman all occurred on Pesach.

At his door You knocked in the heat of the day
                                                            on Passover;
He satiated the angels with matzah-cakes on Passover
And he ran to the herd —
      symbolic of the sacrificial beast   of Passover.
      And you shall say: This is the feast of Passover.
The Sodomites provoked (God)
      and were devoured by fire   on Passover;
Lot was withdrawn from them —
      he had baked matzos at the time   of Passover.
You swept clean the soil of Moph and Noph (in Egypt)
      when You passed through   on Passover.
      And you shall say: This is the feast of Passover.
God, You crushed every first-born of On (in Egypt)
      on the watchful night   of Passover.
But Master — Your own first-born,
      You skipped by merit of the blood   of Passover,
Not to allow the Destroyer to enter my doors
                                                            on Passover.
      And you shall say: This is the feast of Passover.

81 □ THE FAMILY HAGGADAH

מִסְגֶּרֶת סֻגְּרָה בְּעִתּוֹתֵי   פֶּסַח.

נִשְׁמְדָה מִדְיָן בִּצְלִיל שְׂעוֹרֵי עֹמֶר   פֶּסַח.

שֹׁרְפוּ מִשְׁמַנֵּי פוּל וְלוּד בִּיקַד יְקוֹד   פֶּסַח.

וַאֲמַרְתֶּם זֶבַח פֶּסַח:

עוֹד הַיּוֹם בְּנֹב לַעֲמוֹד עַד גָּעָה עוֹנַת   פֶּסַח.

פַּס יַד כָּתְבָה לְקַעֲקֵעַ צוּל   בַּפֶּסַח.

צָפֹה הַצָּפִית עָרוֹךְ הַשֻּׁלְחָן   בַּפֶּסַח.

וַאֲמַרְתֶּם זֶבַח פֶּסַח:

קָהָל כִּנְּסָה הֲדַסָּה צוֹם לְשַׁלֵּשׁ   בַּפֶּסַח.

רֹאשׁ מִבֵּית רָשָׁע מָחַצְתָּ בְּעֵץ חֲמִשִּׁים בַּפֶּסַח.

שְׁתֵּי אֵלֶּה רֶגַע תָּבִיא לְעוּצִית   בַּפֶּסַח.

תָּעֹז יָדְךָ וְתָרוּם יְמִינְךָ כְּלֵיל הִתְקַדֶּשׁ חַג פֶּסַח.

וַאֲמַרְתֶּם זֶבַח פֶּסַח:

On both nights continue here:

כִּי לוֹ נָאֶה. כִּי לוֹ יָאֶה:

אַדִּיר בִּמְלוּכָה. בָּחוּר כַּהֲלָכָה. גְּדוּדָיו
יֹאמְרוּ לוֹ. לְךָ וּלְךָ. לְךָ כִּי לְךָ. לְךָ אַף
לְךָ. לְךָ יהוה הַמַּמְלָכָה. כִּי לוֹ נָאֶה. כִּי לוֹ יָאֶה:

דָּגוּל בִּמְלוּכָה. הָדוּר כַּהֲלָכָה. וָתִיקָיו יֹאמְרוּ
לוֹ. לְךָ וּלְךָ. לְךָ כִּי לְךָ. לְךָ אַף לְךָ. לְךָ יהוה
הַמַּמְלָכָה. כִּי לוֹ נָאֶה. כִּי לוֹ יָאֶה:

זַכַּאי בִּמְלוּכָה. חָסִין כַּהֲלָכָה. טַפְסְרָיו יֹאמְרוּ
לוֹ. לְךָ וּלְךָ. לְךָ כִּי לְךָ. לְךָ אַף לְךָ. לְךָ יהוה
הַמַּמְלָכָה. כִּי לוֹ נָאֶה. כִּי לוֹ יָאֶה:

יָחִיד בִּמְלוּכָה. כַּבִּיר כַּהֲלָכָה. לִמּוּדָיו יֹאמְרוּ
לוֹ. לְךָ וּלְךָ. לְךָ כִּי לְךָ. לְךָ אַף לְךָ. לְךָ יהוה
הַמַּמְלָכָה. כִּי לוֹ נָאֶה. כִּי לוֹ יָאֶה:

מוֹשֵׁל בִּמְלוּכָה. נוֹרָא כַּהֲלָכָה. סְבִיבָיו

82 □ הגדה של פסח

The beleaguered (Jericho) was besieged on Passover.
Midian was destroyed with a barley cake,
from the Omer of Passover.
The mighty nobles of Pul and Lud (Assyria) were consumed in a great conflagration on Passover.
And you shall say: This is the feast of Passover.
He (Sennacherib) would have stood that day at Nob,
but for the advent of Passover.
A hand inscribed the destruction
of Zul (Babylon) on Passover,
As the watch was set, and the royal table decked
on Passover.
And you shall say: This is the feast of Passover.
Hadassah (Esther) gathered a congregation
for a three-day fast on Passover.

May you bring the downfall of Edom, show the strength which You showed on the night of Pesach, and redeem us as in days of old.

You caused the head of the evil clan (Haman)
to be hanged on a fifty-cubit gallows on Passover.
Doubly, will You bring in an instant
upon Utsis (Edom) on Passover;
Let Your hand be strong, and Your right arm exalted,
as on that night when You hallowed the festival
of Passover.
And you shall say: This is the feast of Passover.

On both nights continue here:

To Him praise is due!　To Him praise is fitting!

Powerful in majesty, perfectly distinguished, His
companies of angels say to him: Yours and only
Yours; Yours, yes Yours; Yours, surely Yours; Yours,
HASHEM, is the sovereignty. To Him praise is due! To
Him praise is fitting!

We cannot possibly list all of God's praises for He and His praises are infinite. It has become the practice to use an alphabetical ordering of praise, as if to say, "We praise You in every way which starts with the letter aleph, or beis, or gimmel ... from the beginning of the alphabet to the end."

Supreme in kingship, perfectly glorious, His faithful
say to Him: Yours and only Yours; Yours, yes Yours;
Yours, surely Yours; Yours, HASHEM, is the sovereignty.
To Him praise is due! To Him praise is fitting!

Pure in kingship, perfectly mighty, His angels say
unto him: Yours and only Yours; Yours, yes Yours;
Yours, surely Yours; Yours, HASHEM, is the sovereignty.
To Him praise is due! To Him praise is fitting!

Alone in kingship, perfectly omnipotent, His
scholars say unto Him: Yours and only Yours; Yours,
yes Yours; Yours, surely Yours; Yours, HASHEM, is the
sovereignty. To Him praise is due! To Him praise is fitting!

Commanding in kingship, perfectly wondrous, His

83 □ THE FAMILY HAGGADAH

יאמְרוּ לוֹ. לְךָ וּלְךָ. לְךָ כִּי לְךָ. לְךָ אַף לְךָ. לְךָ
יהוה הַמַּמְלָכָה. כִּי לוֹ נָאֶה. כִּי לוֹ יָאֶה:

עָנָיו בִּמְלוּכָה. פּוֹדֶה כַּהֲלָכָה. צַדִּיקָיו יאמְרוּ
לוֹ. לְךָ וּלְךָ. לְךָ כִּי לְךָ. לְךָ אַף לְךָ. לְךָ יהוה
הַמַּמְלָכָה. כִּי לוֹ נָאֶה. כִּי לוֹ יָאֶה:

קָדוֹשׁ בִּמְלוּכָה. רַחוּם כַּהֲלָכָה. שִׁנְאַנָיו
יאמְרוּ לוֹ. לְךָ וּלְךָ. לְךָ כִּי לְךָ. לְךָ אַף לְךָ. לְךָ
יהוה הַמַּמְלָכָה. כִּי לוֹ נָאֶה. כִּי לוֹ יָאֶה:

תַּקִּיף בִּמְלוּכָה. תּוֹמֵךְ כַּהֲלָכָה. תְּמִימָיו
יאמְרוּ לוֹ. לְךָ וּלְךָ. לְךָ כִּי לְךָ. לְךָ אַף לְךָ. לְךָ
יהוה הַמַּמְלָכָה. כִּי לוֹ נָאֶה. כִּי לוֹ יָאֶה:

אַדִּיר הוּא יִבְנֶה בֵיתוֹ בְּקָרוֹב. בִּמְהֵרָה
בִּמְהֵרָה בְּיָמֵינוּ בְּקָרוֹב. אֵל
בְּנֵה אֵל בְּנֵה. בְּנֵה בֵיתְךָ בְּקָרוֹב:

בָּחוּר הוּא. גָּדוֹל הוּא. דָּגוּל הוּא. יִבְנֶה בֵיתוֹ
בְּקָרוֹב. בִּמְהֵרָה בִּמְהֵרָה בְּיָמֵינוּ בְּקָרוֹב. אֵל
בְּנֵה אֵל בְּנֵה. בְּנֵה בֵיתְךָ בְּקָרוֹב:

הָדוּר הוּא. וָתִיק הוּא. זַכַּאי הוּא. חָסִיד הוּא.
יִבְנֶה בֵיתוֹ בְּקָרוֹב. בִּמְהֵרָה בִּמְהֵרָה בְּיָמֵינוּ
בְּקָרוֹב. אֵל בְּנֵה אֵל בְּנֵה. בְּנֵה בֵיתְךָ בְּקָרוֹב:

טָהוֹר הוּא. יָחִיד הוּא. כַּבִּיר הוּא. לָמוּד
הוּא. מֶלֶךְ הוּא. נוֹרָא הוּא. סַגִּיב הוּא. עִזּוּז
הוּא. פּוֹדֶה הוּא. צַדִּיק הוּא. יִבְנֶה בֵיתוֹ בְּקָרוֹב.
בִּמְהֵרָה בִּמְהֵרָה בְּיָמֵינוּ בְּקָרוֹב. אֵל בְּנֵה אֵל
בְּנֵה. בְּנֵה בֵיתְךָ בְּקָרוֹב.

קָדוֹשׁ הוּא. רַחוּם הוּא. שַׁדַּי הוּא. תַּקִּיף
הוּא. יִבְנֶה בֵיתוֹ בְּקָרוֹב. בִּמְהֵרָה בִּמְהֵרָה
בְּיָמֵינוּ בְּקָרוֹב. אֵל בְּנֵה אֵל בְּנֵה. בְּנֵה בֵיתְךָ
בְּקָרוֹב:

surrounding (angels) say to Him: Yours and only Yours; Yours, yes Yours; Yours, surely Yours; Yours, HASHEM, is the sovereignty. To Him praise is due! To Him praise is fitting!

Gentle in Kingship, perfectly the Redeemer, His righteous say to Him: Yours and only Yours; Yours, yes Yours; Yours, surely Yours; Yours, HASHEM, is the sovereignty. To Him praise is due! To Him praise is fitting!

Holy in kingship, perfectly merciful, His troops of angels say to Him: Yours and only Yours; Yours, yes Yours; Yours, surely Yours; Yours, HASHEM, is the sovereignty. To Him praise is due! To Him praise is fitting!

Almighty in kingship, perfectly sustaining, His perfect ones say to Him: Yours and only Yours; Yours, yes Yours; Yours, surely Yours; Yours, HASHEM, is the sovereignty. To Him praise is due! To Him praise is fitting!

He is most mighty. May He soon rebuild His House, speedily, yes speedily, in our days, soon. God, rebuild, God, rebuild, rebuild Your House soon!

He is distinguished, He is great, He is exalted. May He soon rebuild His House, speedily, yes speedily, in our days, soon. God, rebuild, God, rebuild, rebuild Your House soon!

A hymn of our fervent desire for the Messianic age and the rebuilt Temple. The Sages teach that the Third Temple will not be built by man but will descend from heaven at the time of the redemption, for this reason we ask that "He soon rebuild His House."

He is all glorious, He is faithful, He is faultless, He is righteous. May He soon rebuild His House, speedily, yes speedily, in our days, soon. God, rebuild, God, rebuild, rebuild Your House soon!

He is pure, He is unique, He is powerful, He is all-wise, He is King, He is awesome, He is sublime, He is all-powerful, He is the Redeemer, He is the all-righteous. May He soon rebuild His House, speedily, yes speedily, in our days, soon. God, rebuild, God, rebuild, rebuild Your House soon!

He is holy, He is compassionate, He is Almighty, He is omnipotent. May He soon rebuild His House, speedily, yes speedily, in our days, soon. God, rebuild, God, rebuild, rebuild Your House soon!

אֶחָד מִי יוֹדֵעַ. אֶחָד אֲנִי יוֹדֵעַ. אֶחָד
אֱלֹהֵינוּ שֶׁבַּשָּׁמַיִם וּבָאָרֶץ:

שְׁנַיִם מִי יוֹדֵעַ. שְׁנַיִם אֲנִי יוֹדֵעַ. שְׁנֵי לֻחוֹת
הַבְּרִית. אֶחָד אֱלֹהֵינוּ שֶׁבַּשָּׁמַיִם וּבָאָרֶץ:

שְׁלֹשָׁה מִי יוֹדֵעַ. שְׁלֹשָׁה אֲנִי יוֹדֵעַ. שְׁלֹשָׁה
אָבוֹת. שְׁנֵי לֻחוֹת הַבְּרִית. אֶחָד אֱלֹהֵינוּ
שֶׁבַּשָּׁמַיִם וּבָאָרֶץ:

אַרְבַּע מִי יוֹדֵעַ. אַרְבַּע אֲנִי יוֹדֵעַ. אַרְבַּע
אִמָּהוֹת. שְׁלֹשָׁה אָבוֹת. שְׁנֵי לֻחוֹת הַבְּרִית.
אֶחָד אֱלֹהֵינוּ שֶׁבַּשָּׁמַיִם וּבָאָרֶץ:

חֲמִשָּׁה מִי יוֹדֵעַ. חֲמִשָּׁה אֲנִי יוֹדֵעַ. חֲמִשָּׁה
חֻמְשֵׁי תוֹרָה. אַרְבַּע אִמָּהוֹת. שְׁלֹשָׁה אָבוֹת.
שְׁנֵי לֻחוֹת הַבְּרִית. אֶחָד אֱלֹהֵינוּ שֶׁבַּשָּׁמַיִם
וּבָאָרֶץ:

שִׁשָּׁה מִי יוֹדֵעַ. שִׁשָּׁה אֲנִי יוֹדֵעַ. שִׁשָּׁה סִדְרֵי
מִשְׁנָה. חֲמִשָּׁה חֻמְשֵׁי תוֹרָה. אַרְבַּע אִמָּהוֹת.
שְׁלֹשָׁה אָבוֹת. שְׁנֵי לֻחוֹת הַבְּרִית. אֶחָד אֱלֹהֵינוּ
שֶׁבַּשָּׁמַיִם וּבָאָרֶץ:

שִׁבְעָה מִי יוֹדֵעַ. שִׁבְעָה אֲנִי יוֹדֵעַ. שִׁבְעָה יְמֵי
שַׁבַּתָּא. שִׁשָּׁה סִדְרֵי מִשְׁנָה. חֲמִשָּׁה חֻמְשֵׁי
תוֹרָה. אַרְבַּע אִמָּהוֹת. שְׁלֹשָׁה אָבוֹת. שְׁנֵי
לֻחוֹת הַבְּרִית. אֶחָד אֱלֹהֵינוּ שֶׁבַּשָּׁמַיִם וּבָאָרֶץ:

שְׁמוֹנָה מִי יוֹדֵעַ. שְׁמוֹנָה אֲנִי יוֹדֵעַ. שְׁמוֹנָה
יְמֵי מִילָה. שִׁבְעָה יְמֵי שַׁבַּתָּא. שִׁשָּׁה סִדְרֵי
מִשְׁנָה. חֲמִשָּׁה חֻמְשֵׁי תוֹרָה. אַרְבַּע אִמָּהוֹת.
שְׁלֹשָׁה אָבוֹת. שְׁנֵי לֻחוֹת הַבְּרִית. אֶחָד אֱלֹהֵינוּ
שֶׁבַּשָּׁמַיִם וּבָאָרֶץ:

תִּשְׁעָה מִי יוֹדֵעַ. תִּשְׁעָה אֲנִי יוֹדֵעַ. תִּשְׁעָה
יַרְחֵי לֵדָה. שְׁמוֹנָה יְמֵי מִילָה. שִׁבְעָה יְמֵי

קַדֵּשׁ
KADDESH

וּרְחַץ
URECHATZ

כַּרְפַּס
KARPAS

יַחַץ
YACHATZ

מַגִּיד
MAGGID

רָחְצָה
RACHTZAH

מוֹצִיא
MOTZI

מַצָּה
MATZAH

מָרוֹר
MAROR

כּוֹרֵךְ
KORECH

שֻׁלְחָן
עוֹרֵךְ
SHULCHAN
ORECH

צָפוּן
TZAFUN

בָּרֵךְ
BARECH

הַלֵּל
HALLEL

נִרְצָה
NIRTZAH

86 ☐ הגדה של פסח

Who Knows One?

By what merits were our ancestors redeemed from Egypt?

Who knows one? I know one: One is our God, in heaven and on earth.

They believed in the One God ...

Who knows two? I know two: two are the Tablets of the Covenant; One is our God, in heaven and on earth.

and were eager to accept the two Tablets.

Who knows three? I know three: three are the Patriarchs; two are the Tablets of the Covenant; One is our God, in heaven and on earth.

God had promised the three Patriarchs — Abraham, Isaac, Jacob — that He would redeem their children.

Who knows four? I know four: four are the Matriarchs; three are the Patriarchs; two are the Tablets of the Covenant; One is our God, in heaven and on earth.

The Israelite women followed the way of modest righteousness taught them by the four Matriarchs — Sarah, Rebecca, Rachel, Leah.

Who knows five? I know five: five are the books of Torah; four are the Matriarchs; three are the Patriarchs; two are the Tablets of the Covenant; One is our God, in heaven and on earth.

They would soon receive the Five Books of Moses, which form the core of the Written Torah,

Who knows six? I know six: six are the Orders of the Mishnah; five are the books of Torah; four are the Matriarchs; three are the Patriarchs; two are the Tablets of the Covenant; One is our God, in heaven and on earth.

and the Oral Torah comprising the six sections of the Mishnah.

Who knows seven? I know seven: seven are the days of the week; six are the Orders of the Mishnah; five are the books of the Torah; four are the Matriarchs; three are the Patriarchs; two are the Tablets of the Covenant; One is our God, in heaven and on earth.

Even during their period of slavery, they chose the seventh day as their day of rest.

Who knows eight? I know eight: eight are the days of circumcision; seven are the days of the week; six are the Orders of the Mishnah; five are the books of Torah; four are the Matriarchs; three are the Patriarchs; two are the Tablets of the Covenant; One is our God, in heaven and on the earth.

Circumcision, usually done on the eighth day of life, was performed en mass on the eve of the Exodus.

Who knows nine? I know nine: nine are the months of pregnancy; eight are the days of circumcision;

לְחַיֵי הָעוֹלָם הַבָּא שֶׁכֻּלוֹ שַׁבָּת וּמְנוּחָה לְחַיֵי הָעוֹלָמִים. מִגְדוֹל יְשׁוּעוֹת מַלְכּוֹ וְעֹשֶׂה חֶסֶד לִמְשִׁיחוֹ לְדָוִד וּלְזַרְעוֹ עַד עוֹלָם. עֹשֶׂה שָׁלוֹם בִּמְרוֹמָיו הוּא יַעֲשֶׂה שָׁלוֹם עָלֵינוּ וְעַל כָּל יִשְׂרָאֵל וְאִמְרוּ אָמֵן. יְראוּ אֶת יְיָ קְדֹשָׁיו כִּי אֵין מַחְסוֹר לִירֵאָיו. כְּפִירִים רָשׁוּ וְרָעֵבוּ וְדֹרְשֵׁי יְיָ לֹא יַחְסְרוּ כָל טוֹב. הוֹדוּ לַיְיָ כִּי טוֹב כִּי לְעוֹלָם חַסְדּוֹ.

פּוֹתֵחַ אֶת יָדֶךָ וּמַשְׂבִּיעַ לְכָל חַי רָצוֹן: בָּרוּךְ הַגֶּבֶר אֲשֶׁר יִבְטַח בַּייָ וְהָיָה יְיָ מִבְטַחוֹ. נַעַר הָיִיתִי גַּם זָקַנְתִּי וְלֹא רָאִיתִי צַדִּיק נֶעֱזָב וְזַרְעוֹ מְבַקֶּשׁ לָחֶם. יְיָ עֹז לְעַמּוֹ יִתֵּן יְיָ יְבָרֵךְ אֶת עַמּוֹ בַשָּׁלוֹם.

seven are the days of the week; six are the Orders of the Mishnah; five are the books of the Torah; four are the Matriarchs; three are the Patriarchs; two are the Tablets of the Covenant; One is our God, in heaven and on the earth.

Who knows ten? I know ten: ten are the Ten Commandments; nine are the months of pregnancy; eight are the days of circumcision; seven are the days of the week; six are the Orders of the Mishnah; five are the books of the Torah; four are the Matriarchs; three are the Patriarchs; two are the Tablets of the Covenant; One is our God, in heaven and on earth.

Who knows eleven? I know eleven: eleven are the stars (in Joseph's dream); ten are the Ten Commandments; nine are the months of pregnancy; eight are the days of circumcision; seven are the days of the week; six are the Orders of the Mishnah; five are the books of the Torah; four are the Matriarchs; three are the Patriarchs; two are the Tablets of the Covenant; One is our God, in heaven and on earth.

Who knows twelve? I know twelve: twelve are the tribes; eleven are the stars (in Joseph's dream); ten are the Ten Commandments; nine are the months of pregnancy; eight are the days of circumcision; seven are the days of the week; six are the Orders of the Mishnah; five are the books of the Torah; four are the Matriarchs; three are the Patriarchs; two are the Tablets of the Covenant; One is our God, in heaven and on earth.

Who knows thirteen? I know thirteen: thirteen are the attributes of God; twelve are the tribes; eleven are the stars (in Joseph's dream); ten are the Ten Commandments; nine are the months of pregnancy; eight are the days of circumcision; seven are the days of the week; six are the Orders of the Mishnah; five are the books of the Torah; four are the Matriarchs; three are the Patriarchs; two are the Tablets of the Covenant; One is our God, in heaven and on earth.

The Jewish wives were not intimidated by Pharaoh's orders to "cast every son … into the river," but conceived and carried for the full nine months, placing their trust in God's salvation.

The nation would imminently accept the Ten Commandments.

The families of Joseph's eleven brothers, represented by the stars in his dream, changed neither their names, language, nor manner of dress in Egypt. (As viceroy, Joseph was given an official name and royal wardrobe by Pharaoh, and spoke the language of the court.)

All twelve tribes maintained their familial integrity, for no Jewish woman consented to the advances of the Egyptian taskmasters.

God taught Moses the prayer of the Thirteen Attributes of Divine Mercy, to be followed in word and deed, in times of national distress.

89 □ THE FAMILY HAGGADAH

חַד גַּדְיָא. חַד גַּדְיָא. דְּזַבִּין אַבָּא בִּתְרֵי
זוּזֵי. חַד גַּדְיָא חַד גַּדְיָא:

וְאָתָא **שׁוּנְרָא** וְאָכְלָה לְגַדְיָא. דְּזַבִּין אַבָּא
בִּתְרֵי זוּזֵי. חַד גַּדְיָא חַד גַּדְיָא:

וְאָתָא **כַלְבָּא** וְנָשַׁךְ לְשׁוּנְרָא. דְּאָכְלָא לְגַדְיָא.
דְּזַבִּין אַבָּא בִּתְרֵי זוּזֵי. חַד גַּדְיָא חַד גַּדְיָא:

וְאָתָא **חוּטְרָא** וְהִכָּה לְכַלְבָּא. דְּנָשַׁךְ
לְשׁוּנְרָא. דְּאָכְלָה לְגַדְיָא. דְּזַבִּין אַבָּא בִּתְרֵי זוּזֵי.
חַד גַּדְיָא חַד גַּדְיָא:

וְאָתָא **נוּרָא** וְשָׂרַף לְחוּטְרָא. דְּהִכָּה לְכַלְבָּא.
דְּנָשַׁךְ לְשׁוּנְרָא. דְּאָכְלָה לְגַדְיָא. דְּזַבִּין אַבָּא
בִּתְרֵי זוּזֵי. חַד גַּדְיָא חַד גַּדְיָא:

וְאָתָא **מַיָּא** וְכָבָה לְנוּרָא. דְּשָׂרַף לְחוּטְרָא.
דְּהִכָּה לְכַלְבָּא. דְּנָשַׁךְ לְשׁוּנְרָא. דְּאָכְלָה לְגַדְיָא.
דְּזַבִּין אַבָּא בִּתְרֵי זוּזֵי. חַד גַּדְיָא חַד גַּדְיָא:

וְאָתָא **תוֹרָא** וְשָׁתָה לְמַיָּא. דְּכָבָה לְנוּרָא.
דְּשָׂרַף לְחוּטְרָא. דְּהִכָּה לְכַלְבָּא. דְּנָשַׁךְ
לְשׁוּנְרָא. דְּאָכְלָה לְגַדְיָא. דְּזַבִּין אַבָּא בִּתְרֵי זוּזֵי.
חַד גַּדְיָא חַד גַּדְיָא:

וְאָתָא **הַשּׁוֹחֵט** וְשָׁחַט לְתוֹרָא. דְּשָׁתָא לְמַיָּא.
דְּכָבָה לְנוּרָא. דְּשָׂרַף לְחוּטְרָא. דְּהִכָּה לְכַלְבָּא.
דְּנָשַׁךְ לְשׁוּנְרָא. דְּאָכְלָה לְגַדְיָא. דְּזַבִּין אַבָּא
בִּתְרֵי זוּזֵי. חַד גַּדְיָא חַד גַּדְיָא:

וְאָתָא **מַלְאַךְ הַמָּוֶת** וְשָׁחַט לְשׁוֹחֵט. דְּשָׁחַט
לְתוֹרָא. דְּשָׁתָה לְמַיָּא. דְּכָבָה לְנוּרָא. דְּשָׂרַף
לְחוּטְרָא. דְּהִכָּה לְכַלְבָּא. דְּנָשַׁךְ לְשׁוּנְרָא.
דְּאָכְלָה לְגַדְיָא. דְּזַבִּין אַבָּא בִּתְרֵי זוּזֵי. חַד גַּדְיָא
חַד גַּדְיָא:

וְאָתָא **הַקָּדוֹשׁ בָּרוּךְ הוּא** וְשָׁחַט לְמַלְאַךְ

A kid, a kid, that father bought for two zuzim, a kid, a kid.

A cat then came and devoured the kid that father bought for two zuzim, a kid, a kid.

A dog then came and bit the cat, that devoured the kid that father bought for two zuzim, a kid, a kid.

A stick then came, and beat the dog, that bit the cat, that devoured the kid that father bought for two zuzim, a kid, a kid.

A fire then came and burnt the stick, that beat the dog, that bit the cat, that devoured the kid that father bought for two zuzim, a kid, a kid.

Water then came and quenched the fire, that burnt the stick, that beat the dog, that bit the cat, that devoured the kid that father bought for two zuzim, a kid, a kid.

An ox then came, and drank the water, that quenched the fire, that burnt the stick, that beat the dog, that bit the cat, that devoured the kid that father bought for two zuzim, a kid, a kid.

A slaughterer then came, and slaughtered the ox, that drank the water, that quenched the fire, that burnt the stick, that beat the dog, that bit the cat, that devoured the kid that father bought for two zuzim, a kid, a kid.

The angel of death then came and killed the slaughterer, who slaughtered the ox, that drank the water, that quenched the fire, that burnt the stick, that beat the dog, that bit the cat, that devoured the kid that father bought for two zuzim, a kid, a kid.

The Holy One, blessed is He, then came and slew the angel of death, who killed the slaughterer, who

Lest one feel, God forbid, that the events of the Exodus are overshadowed by the centuries-long night of the present exile, and seek respite in some lifestyle inconsistent with that prescribed by the Torah, the Haggadah closes with the soliloquy of a lost soul seeking to identify with a higher truth. "The goat supplies my needs — meat, milk, leather, mohair, tent skins — perhaps it is divine! But the cat can easily devour the baby goat — shall I worship the cat? Or the dog that can overpower the cat? ..."

In like fashion he eliminates worship of brute strength (stick, ox), deification of the elements (fire, water), idolization of man (slaughterer), and adoration of angels. The supremacy of the Holy One, Blessed is He, and the subservience of all of Creation to Him is thus arrived at as the ultimate truth.

91 □ THE FAMILY HAGGADAH

הַמָּוֶת. דְּשָׁחַט לְשׁוֹחֵט. דְּשָׁחַט לְתוֹרָא. דְּשָׁתָה לְמַיָּא. דְּכָבָה לְנוּרָא. דְּשָׂרַף לְחוּטְרָא. דְּהִכָּה לְכַלְבָּא. דְּנָשַׁךְ לְשׁוּנְרָא. דְּאָכְלָה לְגַדְיָא. דְּזַבִּין אַבָּא בִּתְרֵי זוּזֵי. חַד גַּדְיָא חַד גַּדְיָא:

slaughtered the ox, that drank the water, that quenched the fire, that burnt the stick, that beat the dog, that bit the cat, that devoured the kid that father bought for two zuzim, a kid a kid.

Although the Haggadah formally ends at this point, one should continue to occupy himself with the story of the Exodus, and the laws of Passover, until sleep overtakes him. Many recite Song of Songs after the Haggadah.

שיר השירים

🔊 Shir HaShirim / Song of Songs*

א

שִׁיר הַשִּׁירִים אֲשֶׁר לִשְׁלֹמֹה: יִשָּׁקֵנִי מִנְּשִׁיקוֹת פִּיהוּ כִּי־טוֹבִים דֹּדֶיךָ מִיָּיִן: לְרֵיחַ שְׁמָנֶיךָ טוֹבִים שֶׁמֶן תּוּרַק שְׁמֶךָ עַל־כֵּן עֲלָמוֹת אֲהֵבוּךָ: מָשְׁכֵנִי אַחֲרֶיךָ נָּרוּצָה הֱבִיאַנִי הַמֶּלֶךְ חֲדָרָיו נָגִילָה וְנִשְׂמְחָה בָּךְ נַזְכִּירָה דֹדֶיךָ מִיַּיִן מֵישָׁרִים אֲהֵבוּךָ: שְׁחוֹרָה אֲנִי וְנָאוָה בְּנוֹת יְרוּשָׁלָ͏ִם כְּאָהֳלֵי קֵדָר כִּירִיעוֹת שְׁלֹמֹה: אַל־תִּרְאֻנִי שֶׁאֲנִי שְׁחַרְחֹרֶת שֶׁשְּׁזָפַתְנִי הַשָּׁמֶשׁ בְּנֵי אִמִּי נִחֲרוּ־בִי שָׂמֻנִי נֹטֵרָה אֶת־הַכְּרָמִים כַּרְמִי שֶׁלִּי לֹא נָטָרְתִּי: הַגִּידָה לִּי שֶׁאָהֲבָה נַפְשִׁי אֵיכָה תִרְעֶה אֵיכָה תַּרְבִּיץ בַּצָּהֳרָיִם שַׁלָּמָה אֶהְיֶה כְּעֹטְיָה עַל עֶדְרֵי חֲבֵרֶיךָ: אִם־לֹא תֵדְעִי לָךְ הַיָּפָה בַּנָּשִׁים צְאִי־לָךְ בְּעִקְבֵי הַצֹּאן וּרְעִי אֶת־גְּדִיֹּתַיִךְ עַל מִשְׁכְּנוֹת הָרֹעִים: לְסֻסָתִי בְּרִכְבֵי פַרְעֹה דִּמִּיתִיךְ רַעְיָתִי: נָאווּ לְחָיַיִךְ בַּתֹּרִים צַוָּארֵךְ בַּחֲרוּזִים: תּוֹרֵי זָהָב נַעֲשֶׂה־לָּךְ עִם נְקֻדּוֹת הַכָּסֶף: עַד־שֶׁהַמֶּלֶךְ בִּמְסִבּוֹ נִרְדִּי נָתַן רֵיחוֹ: צְרוֹר הַמֹּר | דּוֹדִי לִי בֵּין שָׁדַי יָלִין: אֶשְׁכֹּל הַכֹּפֶר דּוֹדִי לִי בְּכַרְמֵי עֵין גֶּדִי: הִנָּךְ יָפָה רַעְיָתִי הִנָּךְ יָפָה עֵינַיִךְ יוֹנִים: הִנְּךָ יָפֶה דוֹדִי אַף נָעִים אַף־עַרְשֵׂנוּ רַעֲנָנָה: קֹרוֹת בָּתֵּינוּ אֲרָזִים רַהִיטֵנוּ בְּרוֹתִים:

ב

אֲנִי חֲבַצֶּלֶת הַשָּׁרוֹן שׁוֹשַׁנַּת הָעֲמָקִים: כְּשׁוֹשַׁנָּה בֵּין הַחוֹחִים כֵּן רַעְיָתִי בֵּין הַבָּנוֹת: כְּתַפּוּחַ בַּעֲצֵי הַיַּעַר כֵּן דּוֹדִי בֵּין הַבָּנִים בְּצִלּוֹ חִמַּדְתִּי וְיָשַׁבְתִּי וּפִרְיוֹ מָתוֹק לְחִכִּי: הֱבִיאַנִי אֶל־בֵּית הַיַּיִן וְדִגְלוֹ עָלַי אַהֲבָה: סַמְּכוּנִי בָּאֲשִׁישׁוֹת רַפְּדוּנִי בַּתַּפּוּחִים כִּי־חוֹלַת אַהֲבָה אָנִי: שְׂמֹאלוֹ תַּחַת לְרֹאשִׁי וִימִינוֹ תְּחַבְּקֵנִי: הִשְׁבַּעְתִּי אֶתְכֶם בְּנוֹת יְרוּשָׁלַ͏ִם בִּצְבָאוֹת אוֹ בְּאַיְלוֹת הַשָּׂדֶה אִם־תָּעִירוּ | וְאִם־תְּעוֹרְרוּ אֶת־הָאַהֲבָה עַד שֶׁתֶּחְפָּץ: קוֹל דּוֹדִי הִנֵּה־זֶה בָּא מְדַלֵּג עַל־הֶהָרִים מְקַפֵּץ עַל־הַגְּבָעוֹת: דּוֹמֶה דוֹדִי לִצְבִי אוֹ לְעֹפֶר הָאַיָּלִים הִנֵּה־זֶה עוֹמֵד אַחַר כָּתְלֵנוּ מַשְׁגִּיחַ מִן־הַחַלֹּנוֹת מֵצִיץ מִן־הַחֲרַכִּים: עָנָה דוֹדִי וְאָמַר לִי קוּמִי לָךְ רַעְיָתִי יָפָתִי וּלְכִי־לָךְ: כִּי־הִנֵּה הַסְּתָו עָבָר הַגֶּשֶׁם חָלַף הָלַךְ לוֹ: הַנִּצָּנִים נִרְאוּ בָאָרֶץ עֵת הַזָּמִיר הִגִּיעַ וְקוֹל הַתּוֹר נִשְׁמַע בְּאַרְצֵנוּ: הַתְּאֵנָה חָנְטָה פַגֶּיהָ וְהַגְּפָנִים | סְמָדַר נָתְנוּ רֵיחַ קוּמִי לָךְ רַעְיָתִי יָפָתִי וּלְכִי־לָךְ: יוֹנָתִי בְּחַגְוֵי הַסֶּלַע בְּסֵתֶר הַמַּדְרֵגָה הַרְאִינִי אֶת־מַרְאַיִךְ הַשְׁמִיעִנִי אֶת־קוֹלֵךְ כִּי־קוֹלֵךְ עָרֵב וּמַרְאֵיךְ נָאוֶה: אֶחֱזוּ־לָנוּ שׁוּעָלִים שׁוּעָלִים קְטַנִּים מְחַבְּלִים כְּרָמִים וּכְרָמֵינוּ סְמָדַר: דּוֹדִי לִי וַאֲנִי לוֹ הָרֹעֶה בַּשּׁוֹשַׁנִּים: עַד שֶׁיָּפוּחַ הַיּוֹם וְנָסוּ הַצְּלָלִים סֹב דְּמֵה־לְךָ דוֹדִי לִצְבִי אוֹ לְעֹפֶר הָאַיָּלִים עַל־הָרֵי בָתֶר:

ג

עַל־מִשְׁכָּבִי בַּלֵּילוֹת בִּקַּשְׁתִּי אֵת שֶׁאָהֲבָה נַפְשִׁי בִּקַּשְׁתִּיו וְלֹא מְצָאתִיו: אָקוּמָה נָּא וַאֲסוֹבְבָה בָעִיר בַּשְּׁוָקִים וּבָרְחֹבוֹת אֲבַקְשָׁה אֵת שֶׁאָהֲבָה נַפְשִׁי בִּקַּשְׁתִּיו וְלֹא מְצָאתִיו: מְצָאוּנִי הַשֹּׁמְרִים הַסֹּבְבִים בָּעִיר אֵת שֶׁאָהֲבָה נַפְשִׁי רְאִיתֶם: כִּמְעַט שֶׁעָבַרְתִּי מֵהֶם עַד שֶׁמָּצָאתִי אֵת שֶׁאָהֲבָה נַפְשִׁי אֲחַזְתִּיו וְלֹא אַרְפֶּנּוּ עַד־שֶׁהֲבֵיאתִיו אֶל־בֵּית אִמִּי וְאֶל־חֶדֶר הוֹרָתִי: הִשְׁבַּעְתִּי אֶתְכֶם בְּנוֹת יְרוּשָׁלַ͏ִם

---

* For an allegorical translation and anthology of commentaries on Shir HaShirim, the reader is directed to the ArtScroll Tanach Series edition.

93 □ THE FAMILY HAGGADAH

בִּצְבָאוֹת אוֹ בְּאַיְלוֹת הַשָּׂדֶה אִם־תָּעִירוּ | וְאִם־תְּעוֹרְרוּ אֶת־הָאַהֲבָה עַד שֶׁתֶּחְפָּץ:
מִי זֹאת עֹלָה מִן־הַמִּדְבָּר כְּתִימְרוֹת עָשָׁן מְקֻטֶּרֶת מוֹר וּלְבוֹנָה מִכֹּל
אַבְקַת רוֹכֵל: הִנֵּה מִטָּתוֹ שֶׁלִּשְׁלֹמֹה שִׁשִּׁים גִּבֹּרִים סָבִיב לָהּ מִגִּבֹּרֵי יִשְׂרָאֵל: כֻּלָּם
אֲחֻזֵי חֶרֶב מְלֻמְּדֵי מִלְחָמָה אִישׁ חַרְבּוֹ עַל־יְרֵכוֹ מִפַּחַד בַּלֵּילוֹת:
אַפִּרְיוֹן עָשָׂה לוֹ הַמֶּלֶךְ שְׁלֹמֹה מֵעֲצֵי הַלְּבָנוֹן: עַמּוּדָיו עָשָׂה כֶסֶף רְפִידָתוֹ זָהָב
מֶרְכָּבוֹ אַרְגָּמָן תּוֹכוֹ רָצוּף אַהֲבָה מִבְּנוֹת יְרוּשָׁלָ͏ִם: צְאֶינָה | וּרְאֶינָה בְּנוֹת צִיּוֹן
בַּמֶּלֶךְ שְׁלֹמֹה בָּעֲטָרָה שֶׁעִטְּרָה־לּוֹ אִמּוֹ בְּיוֹם חֲתֻנָּתוֹ וּבְיוֹם שִׂמְחַת לִבּוֹ:

ד

הִנָּךְ יָפָה רַעְיָתִי הִנָּךְ יָפָה עֵינַיִךְ יוֹנִים מִבַּעַד לְצַמָּתֵךְ שַׂעְרֵךְ כְּעֵדֶר הָעִזִּים
שֶׁגָּלְשׁוּ מֵהַר גִּלְעָד: שִׁנַּיִךְ כְּעֵדֶר הַקְּצוּבוֹת שֶׁעָלוּ מִן־הָרַחְצָה שֶׁכֻּלָּם מַתְאִימוֹת
וְשַׁכֻּלָה אֵין בָּהֶם: כְּחוּט הַשָּׁנִי שִׂפְתוֹתַיִךְ וּמִדְבָּרֵיךְ נָאוֶה כְּפֶלַח הָרִמּוֹן רַקָּתֵךְ
מִבַּעַד לְצַמָּתֵךְ: כְּמִגְדַּל דָּוִיד צַוָּארֵךְ בָּנוּי לְתַלְפִּיּוֹת אֶלֶף הַמָּגֵן תָּלוּי עָלָיו כֹּל
שִׁלְטֵי הַגִּבֹּרִים: שְׁנֵי שָׁדַיִךְ כִּשְׁנֵי עֳפָרִים תְּאוֹמֵי צְבִיָּה הָרֹעִים בַּשּׁוֹשַׁנִּים: עַד
שֶׁיָּפוּחַ הַיּוֹם וְנָסוּ הַצְּלָלִים אֵלֶךְ לִי אֶל־הַר הַמּוֹר וְאֶל־גִּבְעַת הַלְּבוֹנָה: כֻּלָּךְ יָפָה
רַעְיָתִי וּמוּם אֵין בָּךְ:   אִתִּי מִלְּבָנוֹן כַּלָּה אִתִּי מִלְּבָנוֹן תָּבוֹאִי תָּשׁוּרִי |
מֵרֹאשׁ אֲמָנָה מֵרֹאשׁ שְׂנִיר וְחֶרְמוֹן מִמְּעֹנוֹת אֲרָיוֹת מֵהַרְרֵי נְמֵרִים: לִבַּבְתִּנִי
אֲחֹתִי כַלָּה לִבַּבְתִּנִי בְּאַחַת מֵעֵינַיִךְ בְּאַחַד עֲנָק מִצַּוְּרֹנָיִךְ: מַה־יָּפוּ דֹדַיִךְ אֲחֹתִי
כַלָּה מַה־טֹּבוּ דֹדַיִךְ מִיַּיִן וְרֵיחַ שְׁמָנַיִךְ מִכָּל־בְּשָׂמִים: נֹפֶת תִּטֹּפְנָה שִׂפְתוֹתַיִךְ
כַלָּה דְּבַשׁ וְחָלָב תַּחַת לְשׁוֹנֵךְ וְרֵיחַ שַׂלְמֹתַיִךְ כְּרֵיחַ לְבָנוֹן: גַּן | נָעוּל
אֲחֹתִי כַלָּה גַּל נָעוּל מַעְיָן חָתוּם: שְׁלָחַיִךְ פַּרְדֵּס רִמּוֹנִים עִם פְּרִי מְגָדִים כְּפָרִים
עִם־נְרָדִים: נֵרְדְּ | וְכַרְכֹּם קָנֶה וְקִנָּמוֹן עִם כָּל־עֲצֵי לְבוֹנָה מֹר וַאֲהָלוֹת עִם כָּל־
רָאשֵׁי בְשָׂמִים: מַעְיַן גַּנִּים בְּאֵר מַיִם חַיִּים וְנֹזְלִים מִן־לְבָנוֹן: עוּרִי צָפוֹן וּבוֹאִי
תֵימָן הָפִיחִי גַנִּי יִזְּלוּ בְשָׂמָיו יָבֹא דוֹדִי לְגַנּוֹ וְיֹאכַל פְּרִי מְגָדָיו:

ה

בָּאתִי לְגַנִּי אֲחֹתִי כַלָּה אָרִיתִי מוֹרִי עִם־בְּשָׂמִי אָכַלְתִּי יַעְרִי עִם־דִּבְשִׁי שָׁתִיתִי
יֵינִי עִם־חֲלָבִי אִכְלוּ רֵעִים שְׁתוּ וְשִׁכְרוּ דּוֹדִים: אֲנִי יְשֵׁנָה וְלִבִּי עֵר קוֹל |
דּוֹדִי דוֹפֵק פִּתְחִי־לִי אֲחֹתִי רַעְיָתִי יוֹנָתִי תַמָּתִי שֶׁרֹּאשִׁי נִמְלָא־טָל קְוֻצּוֹתַי
רְסִיסֵי לָיְלָה: פָּשַׁטְתִּי אֶת־כֻּתָּנְתִּי אֵיכָכָה אֶלְבָּשֶׁנָּה רָחַצְתִּי אֶת־רַגְלַי אֵיכָכָה
אֲטַנְּפֵם: דּוֹדִי שָׁלַח יָדוֹ מִן־הַחֹר וּמֵעַי הָמוּ עָלָיו: קַמְתִּי אֲנִי לִפְתֹּחַ לְדוֹדִי וְיָדַי
נָטְפוּ־מוֹר וְאֶצְבְּעֹתַי מוֹר עֹבֵר עַל כַּפּוֹת הַמַּנְעוּל: פָּתַחְתִּי אֲנִי לְדוֹדִי וְדוֹדִי חָמַק
עָבָר נַפְשִׁי יָצְאָה בְדַבְּרוֹ בִּקַּשְׁתִּיהוּ וְלֹא מְצָאתִיהוּ קְרָאתִיו וְלֹא עָנָנִי: מְצָאֻנִי
הַשֹּׁמְרִים הַסֹּבְבִים בָּעִיר הִכּוּנִי פְצָעוּנִי נָשְׂאוּ אֶת־רְדִידִי מֵעָלַי שֹׁמְרֵי הַחֹמוֹת:
הִשְׁבַּעְתִּי אֶתְכֶם בְּנוֹת יְרוּשָׁלָ͏ִם אִם־תִּמְצְאוּ אֶת־דּוֹדִי מַה־תַּגִּידוּ לוֹ שֶׁחוֹלַת
אַהֲבָה אָנִי: מַה־דּוֹדֵךְ מִדּוֹד הַיָּפָה בַּנָּשִׁים מַה־דּוֹדֵךְ מִדּוֹד שֶׁכָּכָה הִשְׁבַּעְתָּנוּ:
דּוֹדִי צַח וְאָדוֹם דָּגוּל מֵרְבָבָה: רֹאשׁוֹ כֶּתֶם פָּז קְוֻצּוֹתָיו תַּלְתַּלִּים שְׁחֹרוֹת כָּעוֹרֵב:
עֵינָיו כְּיוֹנִים עַל־אֲפִיקֵי מָיִם רֹחֲצוֹת בֶּחָלָב יֹשְׁבוֹת עַל־מִלֵּאת: לְחָיָו כַּעֲרוּגַת
הַבֹּשֶׂם מִגְדְּלוֹת מֶרְקָחִים שִׂפְתוֹתָיו שׁוֹשַׁנִּים נֹטְפוֹת מוֹר עֹבֵר: יָדָיו גְּלִילֵי זָהָב
מְמֻלָּאִים בַּתַּרְשִׁישׁ מֵעָיו עֶשֶׁת שֵׁן מְעֻלֶּפֶת סַפִּירִים: שׁוֹקָיו עַמּוּדֵי שֵׁשׁ מְיֻסָּדִים
עַל־אַדְנֵי־פָז מַרְאֵהוּ כַּלְּבָנוֹן בָּחוּר כָּאֲרָזִים: חִכּוֹ מַמְתַקִּים וְכֻלּוֹ מַחֲמַדִּים זֶה
דוֹדִי וְזֶה רֵעִי בְּנוֹת יְרוּשָׁלָ͏ִם:

ו

אָנָה הָלַךְ דּוֹדֵךְ הַיָּפָה בַּנָּשִׁים אָנָה פָּנָה דוֹדֵךְ וּנְבַקְשֶׁנּוּ עִמָּךְ: דּוֹדִי יָרַד לְגַנּוֹ
לַעֲרֻגוֹת הַבֹּשֶׂם לִרְעוֹת בַּגַּנִּים וְלִלְקֹט שׁוֹשַׁנִּים: אֲנִי לְדוֹדִי וְדוֹדִי לִי הָרֹעֶה
בַּשׁוֹשַׁנִּים: יָפָה אַתְּ רַעְיָתִי כְּתִרְצָה נָאוָה כִּירוּשָׁלָ͏ִם אֲיֻמָּה כַּנִּדְגָּלוֹת:
הָסֵבִּי עֵינַיִךְ מִנֶּגְדִּי שֶׁהֵם הִרְהִיבֻנִי שַׂעְרֵךְ כְּעֵדֶר הָעִזִּים שֶׁגָּלְשׁוּ מִן-הַגִּלְעָד: שִׁנַּיִךְ
כְּעֵדֶר הָרְחֵלִים שֶׁעָלוּ מִן-הָרַחְצָה שֶׁכֻּלָּם מַתְאִימוֹת וְשַׁכֻּלָה אֵין בָּהֶם: כְּפֶלַח
הָרִמּוֹן רַקָּתֵךְ מִבַּעַד לְצַמָּתֵךְ: שִׁשִּׁים הֵמָּה מְלָכוֹת וּשְׁמֹנִים פִּילַגְשִׁים וַעֲלָמוֹת
אֵין מִסְפָּר: אַחַת הִיא יוֹנָתִי תַמָּתִי אַחַת הִיא לְאִמָּהּ בָּרָה הִיא לְיוֹלַדְתָּהּ רָאוּהָ
בָנוֹת וַיְאַשְּׁרוּהָ מְלָכוֹת וּפִילַגְשִׁים וַיְהַלְלוּהָ: מִי-זֹאת הַנִּשְׁקָפָה כְּמוֹ-
שַׁחַר יָפָה כַלְּבָנָה בָּרָה כַּחַמָּה אֲיֻמָּה כַּנִּדְגָּלוֹת: אֶל-גִּנַּת אֱגוֹז יָרַדְתִּי לִרְאוֹת
בְּאִבֵּי הַנָּחַל לִרְאוֹת הֲפָרְחָה הַגֶּפֶן הֵנֵצוּ הָרִמֹּנִים: לֹא יָדַעְתִּי נַפְשִׁי שָׂמַתְנִי
מַרְכְּבוֹת עַמִּי נָדִיב:

ז

שׁוּבִי שׁוּבִי הַשּׁוּלַמִּית שׁוּבִי שׁוּבִי וְנֶחֱזֶה-בָּךְ מַה-תֶּחֱזוּ בַּשּׁוּלַמִּית כִּמְחֹלַת
הַמַּחֲנָיִם: מַה-יָּפוּ פְעָמַיִךְ בַּנְּעָלִים בַּת-נָדִיב חַמּוּקֵי יְרֵכַיִךְ כְּמוֹ חֲלָאִים מַעֲשֵׂה יְדֵי
אָמָּן: שָׁרְרֵךְ אַגַּן הַסַּהַר אַל-יֶחְסַר הַמָּזֶג בִּטְנֵךְ עֲרֵמַת חִטִּים סוּגָה בַּשּׁוֹשַׁנִּים: שְׁנֵי
שָׁדַיִךְ כִּשְׁנֵי עֳפָרִים תָּאֳמֵי צְבִיָּה: צַוָּארֵךְ כְּמִגְדַּל הַשֵּׁן עֵינַיִךְ בְּרֵכוֹת בְּחֶשְׁבּוֹן עַל-
שַׁעַר בַּת-רַבִּים אַפֵּךְ כְּמִגְדַּל הַלְּבָנוֹן צוֹפֶה פְּנֵי דַמָּשֶׂק: רֹאשֵׁךְ עָלַיִךְ כַּכַּרְמֶל
וְדַלַּת רֹאשֵׁךְ כָּאַרְגָּמָן מֶלֶךְ אָסוּר בָּרְהָטִים: מַה-יָּפִית וּמַה-נָּעַמְתְּ אַהֲבָה
בַּתַּעֲנוּגִים: זֹאת קוֹמָתֵךְ דָּמְתָה לְתָמָר וְשָׁדַיִךְ לְאַשְׁכֹּלוֹת: אָמַרְתִּי אֶעֱלֶה בְתָמָר
אֹחֲזָה בְּסַנְסִנָּיו וְיִהְיוּ-נָא שָׁדַיִךְ כְּאֶשְׁכְּלוֹת הַגֶּפֶן וְרֵיחַ אַפֵּךְ כַּתַּפּוּחִים: וְחִכֵּךְ כְּיֵין
הַטּוֹב הוֹלֵךְ לְדוֹדִי לְמֵישָׁרִים דּוֹבֵב שִׂפְתֵי יְשֵׁנִים: אֲנִי לְדוֹדִי וְעָלַי תְּשׁוּקָתוֹ: לְכָה
דוֹדִי נֵצֵא הַשָּׂדֶה נָלִינָה בַּכְּפָרִים: נַשְׁכִּימָה לַכְּרָמִים נִרְאֶה אִם פָּרְחָה הַגֶּפֶן פִּתַּח
הַסְּמָדַר הֵנֵצוּ הָרִמּוֹנִים שָׁם אֶתֵּן אֶת-דֹּדַי לָךְ: הַדּוּדָאִים נָתְנוּ-רֵיחַ וְעַל-פְּתָחֵינוּ
כָּל-מְגָדִים חֲדָשִׁים גַּם-יְשָׁנִים דּוֹדִי צָפַנְתִּי לָךְ:

ח

מִי יִתֶּנְךָ כְּאָח לִי יוֹנֵק שְׁדֵי אִמִּי אֶמְצָאֲךָ בַחוּץ אֶשָּׁקְךָ גַּם לֹא-יָבֻזוּ לִי: אֶנְהָגְךָ
אֲבִיאֲךָ אֶל-בֵּית אִמִּי תְּלַמְּדֵנִי אַשְׁקְךָ מִיַּיִן הָרֶקַח מֵעֲסִיס רִמֹּנִי: שְׂמֹאלוֹ תַּחַת
רֹאשִׁי וִימִינוֹ תְּחַבְּקֵנִי: הִשְׁבַּעְתִּי אֶתְכֶם בְּנוֹת יְרוּשָׁלָ͏ִם מַה-תָּעִירוּ וּמַה-תְּעֹרְרוּ
אֶת-הָאַהֲבָה עַד שֶׁתֶּחְפָּץ: מִי זֹאת עֹלָה מִן-הַמִּדְבָּר מִתְרַפֶּקֶת עַל-
דּוֹדָהּ תַּחַת הַתַּפּוּחַ עוֹרַרְתִּיךָ שָׁמָּה חִבְּלַתְךָ אִמֶּךָ שָׁמָּה חִבְּלָה יְלָדַתְךָ: שִׂימֵנִי
כַחוֹתָם עַל-לִבֶּךָ כַּחוֹתָם עַל-זְרוֹעֶךָ כִּי-עַזָּה כַמָּוֶת אַהֲבָה קָשָׁה כִשְׁאוֹל קִנְאָה
רְשָׁפֶיהָ רִשְׁפֵּי אֵשׁ שַׁלְהֶבֶתְיָה: מַיִם רַבִּים לֹא יוּכְלוּ לְכַבּוֹת אֶת-הָאַהֲבָה וּנְהָרוֹת
לֹא יִשְׁטְפוּהָ אִם-יִתֵּן אִישׁ אֶת-כָּל-הוֹן בֵּיתוֹ בָּאַהֲבָה בּוֹז יָבוּזוּ לוֹ:
אָחוֹת לָנוּ קְטַנָּה וְשָׁדַיִם אֵין לָהּ מַה-נַּעֲשֶׂה לַאֲחֹתֵנוּ בַּיּוֹם שֶׁיְּדֻבַּר-בָּהּ: אִם-
חוֹמָה הִיא נִבְנֶה עָלֶיהָ טִירַת כָּסֶף וְאִם-דֶּלֶת הִיא נָצוּר עָלֶיהָ לוּחַ אָרֶז: אֲנִי
חוֹמָה וְשָׁדַי כַּמִּגְדָּלוֹת אָז הָיִיתִי בְעֵינָיו כְּמוֹצְאֵת שָׁלוֹם: כֶּרֶם הָיָה לִשְׁלֹמֹה
בְּבַעַל הָמוֹן נָתַן אֶת-הַכֶּרֶם לַנֹּטְרִים אִישׁ יָבִא בְּפִרְיוֹ אֶלֶף כָּסֶף: כַּרְמִי שֶׁלִּי לְפָנָי
הָאֶלֶף לְךָ שְׁלֹמֹה וּמָאתַיִם לְנֹטְרִים אֶת-פִּרְיוֹ: הַיּוֹשֶׁבֶת בַּגַּנִּים חֲבֵרִים מַקְשִׁיבִים
לְקוֹלֵךְ הַשְׁמִיעִנִי: בְּרַח דּוֹדִי וּדְמֵה-לְךָ לִצְבִי אוֹ לְעֹפֶר הָאַיָּלִים עַל הָרֵי בְשָׂמִים:

95 □ THE FAMILY HAGGADAH

This volume is part of
THE ARTSCROLL SERIES®
an ongoing project of
translations, commentaries and expositions
on Scripture, Mishnah, Talmud, Halachah,
liturgy, history, the classic Rabbinic writings,
biographies, and thought.

For a brochure of current publications
visit your local Hebrew bookseller
or contact the publisher:

Mesorah Publications, ltd

4401 Second Avenue
Brooklyn, New York 11232
(718) 921-9000